JOSHUA, JUDGES, SAMUEL, KINGS

PROCLAMATION COMMENTARIES

•The Old Testament
Witnesses for Preaching

Foster R. McCurley, *Editor*

JOSHUA, JUDGES, SAMUEL, KINGS

Walter E. Rast

FORTRESS PRESS   Philadelphia, Pennsylvania

Library of Congress Cataloging in Publication Data

Rast, Walter E., 1930–
    Joshua, Judges, Samuel, Kings.
    (Proclamation commentaries)
    Bibliography: p.
    Includes index.
    1. Bible. O. T. Former prophets—Criticism, interpretation, etc. 2. D document (Biblical criticism)
I. Title.
BS1286.5.R37   222   78-54559
ISBN 0-8006-0594-2

7116C78   Printed in the United States of America   1-594

For
Joel, Timothy,
Rebekah, *and* Peter

CONTENTS

EDITOR'S FOREWORD

This present volume continues *Proclamation Commentaries—The Old Testament Witnesses for Preaching*. Like its New Testament counterpart, this series is not intended to replace traditional commentaries which analyze books of the Bible pericope by pericope or verse by verse. This six-volume series attempts to provide background material on selected Old Testament books which, among other things, will assist the reader in using *Proclamation: Aids for Interpreting the Lessons of the Church Year*. Material offered in these volumes consists of theological themes from various witnesses or theologians out of Israel's believing community. It is our expectation that this approach—examining characteristic themes and motifs—will enable the modern interpreter to comprehend more clearly and fully a particular pericope which contains or alludes to such a subject. In order to give appropriate emphasis to such issues in the brief form of these volumes, the authors present the results, rather than the detailed arguments, of contemporary scholarship.

On the basis of its concern to address the specific task of preaching and teaching the Word of God to audiences today, this commentary series stresses the theological dilemmas which Old Testament Israel faced and to which her witnesses responded. Accordingly, the historical and political details of Israel's life and that of her ancient Near Eastern neighbors are left to other books. Selected for discussion here are those incidents and issues in Israel's history which have a direct relationship to the theological problems and responses in her existence. Since the Word of God is always addressed to specific and concrete situations in the life of people, the motifs and themes in these commentaries are directed to those selected situations which best exemplify a certain witness's theology.

This volume analyzes the rich and complex story of that author or school called the Deuteronomistic historian. The books of his story—Joshua, Judges, Samuel, and Kings—which comprise one-fifth of the Old Testament span the time from Joshua (about 1200 B.C.) to the days of the exiled King Jehoiachin in the sixth century B.C. During these six hundred years the Israelites experienced radical historical and sociological developments. The people were transformed from migrating clans and loosely organized tribes living on the fringe areas of Canaanite civilization into a confederation of tribes called an amphictyony. After two centuries of such a tribal structure the people were organized into a monarchy which in the days of David and Solomon had all the appropriate trimmings. After Solomon's death, the monarchy was split into northern and southern kingdoms, both of which were destroyed eventually. The Deuteronomist inherited traditions from this long and complex development of Israel's life and welded them into a history with a particular theological viewpoint.

The nature and scope of this history have been interpreted in various ways during the last century. Almost a hundred years ago, Julius Wellhausen in his *Prologomena to the History of Israel* demonstrated that the religious ideas of the Babylonian Exile had been imposed on earlier sources in order to give us our present books of Judges, Samuel, and Kings. These books, he argued, contained early historical narratives which were subjected to a revision or redaction called Deuteronomistic because of its dependence on the Book of Deuteronomy. The Book of Joshua was considered by Wellhausen to be composed by an intertwining of the same source documents which had been traced through the Pentateuch: J, E, D, and P. Thus, largely by literary analysis, Wellhausen and his many successors separated a Hexateuch (Genesis—Joshua) from the remaining Deuteronomistic history (Judges—Kings).

In 1943 Martin Noth changed rather dramatically the understanding of this history's nature and scope. Building upon the work of his teacher Albrecht Alt, who pioneered the way to a geographical and sociological understanding of early Israel, Noth presented the view of a continuous Deuteronomistic history which started with the Book of Deuteronomy and extended through the books of Joshua, Judges,

Samuel, and Kings. He argued that the law book found in 621 B.C. by Josiah's men in the Jerusalem temple was expanded by the addition of Deuteronomy 1—3 in order to serve as the introduction to the long historical corpus. Further, he showed that the sources J, E, and P extend only to the end of the Book of Numbers (with a few verses at the end of Deuteronomy attributed to P). Thus, Noth reduced the Pentateuch (or the larger Hexateuch) to a Tetrateuch and expanded the Deuteronomistic history to include the books of Deuteronomy and Joshua.

Strictly speaking, therefore, this volume could have included the Book of Deuteronomy in order to present the entire historical corpus. That Deuteronomy is not treated here by no means indicates a rejection of Noth's convincing argument; it was simply due to an editorial judgment that Deuteronomy be included in another volume along with the Book of Jeremiah in order to treat the affinities in the language, style, and thought of those two witnesses from the seventh century B.C. (see my foreword in Elizabeth Achtemeier's *Deuteronomy, Jeremiah* in this series). Quite appropriately, however, Professor Walter Rast includes references from Deuteronomy in this volume in order to portray a full picture of the Deuteronomistic historian's theological interests.

Rast takes full advantage of those past studies which have demonstrated the antiquity of many of the sources and concepts used by this historian. He stresses the accuracy and importance of those old traditions. At the same time he goes on to elucidate the theological framework of the historian who presented to his day a history with meaning and urgency. The events of the sixth century B.C.—the exile to Babylon and the destruction of Jerusalem and its temple—caused the historian to view the past in a certain way. Professor Rast captures that urgency and presents it as a lesson for preachers today.

Among the many difficult issues to interpret is the relationship between law and grace in this Deuteronomistic history, particularly as those issues relate to the covenants of promise on the one hand (Abraham and David) and a covenant of responsibility on the other (Sinai). Rast's treatment of this tension is carried out with clarity and with theological precision as he warns against an oversimplification of one view over another.

The author's courage to face difficult questions is evident further by his wrestling with the questions of the holy war "ban" by which Canaanites were to be slaughtered and of the right of Israelites to dispossess other peoples of their lands. While admitting the difficulties for the modern interpreter, Professor Rast demonstrates the positive lessons on transmitting beliefs and on accountability for God's gifts, as they can benefit us today.

Walter Rast is Professor of Theology at Valparaiso University in Indiana. He received his Ph.D. from the University of Chicago Divinity School. His contributions to Old Testament scholarship are unique in the sense that he relates vast archaeological experience to biblical hermeneutics and theology. In fact, much of his archaeological work has concentrated on Iron Age levels, precisely the period of the first segments of the Deuteronomistic History. In addition to articles on archaeology and hermeneutics, he is the author of *Tradition History and the Old Testament* (Fortress, 1972).

Spring 1978   FOSTER R. MCCURLEY
Lutheran Theological Seminary at Philadelphia

AUTHOR'S PREFACE

Happily the adoption by many churches of the new Three-Year Lectionary is providing a greater occasion for readings from the books treated in this study. Anyone who reads Jacques Ellul's collection of sermons based on 2 Kings listed in the bibliography below will have to agree that these books contain many untapped resources for contemporary proclamation. I have written this book with those responsible for such proclamation in mind. Though it is not a book about sermonizing, I nonetheless hope that it may stimulate using in the setting of worship some of the sections treated here. I have also tried to keep in mind lay people in the churches, who might find an engagement with the content of one of ancient Israel's significant historical works a challenging experience. If this book should also find its way to being a resource for cherished friends in the synagogue, I shall indeed be gratified. The university or college student, among whom much of my life is lived, has also been part of my audience while this work was taking shape. Naturally my thoughts owe much to frequent discussion with him or her on the topics presented here.

I wish to record my thanks to the administration of my university for its continuing support, especially to Walter E. Keller, chairman of the Department of Theology at Valparaiso University, and Mrs. Eunice Bailey, departmental secretary. I am grateful for the help given at various points by Dr. Foster R. McCurley, the editor of the series. Finally, I owe a great debt to Terry Page, Anne Cook, and Elizabeth Boehringer, for assistance in typing the manuscript at one stage or another.

WALTER E. RAST

13

CHAPTER ONE

A FRAMEWORK FOR INTERPRETATION

The reader who wishes to gain an intelligent understanding of the books of Joshua, Judges, Samuel, and Kings must make an important decision at the outset. This decision has to do with some basic problems regarding the composition of these books and how the interpretation of them will best proceed. Several alternatives are possible.

Traditionally an approach to the books under consideration has prevailed, which continues to be used by some at present. In this view each of the four large historical books which are the object of this study was seen as a self-contained work, written at a particular time by a single person. The Book of Joshua was assumed to have been written by Joshua himself, or a contemporary of his, since the book came to bear his name and he is the prominent figure in it. Judges was attributed to an unknown figure who, it was assumed, lived during the early days of the monarchy, at the time of Saul or David. Both Samuel and Kings, although again ascribed to unknown authors, were similarly thought to have been compiled by persons in Judah who witnessed the events they recorded.

One consequence of this view was that a certain amount of fragmentation dominated the interpretation. The prevailing view employed an overarching theory of inspiration to provide some kind of unity for what otherwise was a fairly atomized understanding. But it was unsuccessful in comprehending larger theological themes which more recent study shows carry across from one book to another. The outcome was that often the interpretation of these books tended to become didactic or moralistic rather than synthetic. The results for preaching were usually disappointing.

A new alternative came to focus on the historical understanding of these books. This approach was initiated soon after the criticism of the Pentateuch had emerged. At first the criticism of the Pentateuch was extended to these historical books, so that the classical sources of the Pentateuch were traced into the "former prophets." This was especially the case with the Book of Joshua which was taken with the first five books to make up a Hexateuch. But the sources J and E were also pursued into the Book of Judges, and a few found evidences of them also in the earliest strata of the books of Samuel and Kings.

This type of criticism soon was to make a significant breakthrough in the understanding of these books. Such a discovery occurred when the insight emerged that the books classified in the Jewish canon as the "former prophets" reflected a theology and literary style reminiscent of the last book of the Pentateuch, Deuteronomy. Out of this insight, which earlier criticism had already noticed by attributing certain sections of the former prophets to D, there arose a new way of viewing these books. But, differing from the earlier studies, the so-called Deuteronomic elements were seen not just as one strand woven together next to several other strands. Rather, it was observed that these elements belonged to the final framework of the books. In other words, the Deuteronomic features were seen to supply the scaffolding for the great amount of content in these books, which included various narratives and numerous older traditions.

The outcome of this work is that the books of Joshua through Kings have come to be seen not so much as a set of independent books but rather a comprehensive history of ancient Israel compiled by a single author or by a school. To this work was given variously the name Deuteronomistic History, the D-Work, or Deuteronomic History.[1] Since the writer of this history seemed to be deeply influenced by the theological ideas of the core of the Book of Deuteronomy, especially chapters 5—28, the name of the fifth book of the Pentateuch has supplied the title for this historical work.

This understanding of the four large books before us has brought many worthwhile results to the interpretation of these books. It is not surprising, therefore, that it has become widely accepted. Basic to this interpretation is that in the books of Joshua through Kings we find a case where redactional and history-of-tradition study are both applicable and effective. By tracing the way the author made use of older traditions which he molded into a comprehensive historical presentation, we are able to gain a new perspective into the theological significance of this work and its use as a source in contemporary proclamation. In the present study this interpretation is assumed, and its implications are pursued. In order not to encumber the discussion with heavy terminology, we have chosen the designation "D history" for the work itself and "D historian" for the author or authors, a problem which is addressed below.

An attentive reading of Joshua through Kings suggests that the material in these books is so arranged as to present a consistent history of Israel from the time of the conquest to the downfall of the Judean state. Some of the unusual features of the work which become evident are the following. First, a unified theological viewpoint dominates, indicating that the work was produced with a more or less single objective: to understand the factors that led to the dissolution of the kingdom of Israel. In the second place, the work makes frequent use of older documents and traditions in a manner which is distinctive to these books. Thirdly, important periods the historian treats are marked off by speeches, such as those found in Joshua 1 and 24, 1 Samuel 12, and 1 Kings 8. Finally, frequent efforts are made by the historian to trace interconnections between earlier and later events, or between an earlier challenge and the later outcome. The historian sketches these relationships by a scheme of prophecy and fulfillment at which we shall look more closely in Chapter Six. This structuring of the historical tradition within a theological framework and interpretation provides a distinctive unity to the work.

We shall examine various places throughout this work where the D historian's use of older traditions can be seen. Here one example is presented to illustrate his redaction of older material, as well as the way in which his usage of earlier material puts a special stamp on a text or tradition. The example chosen for illustration is Joshua 11, an account devoted to the conquest. This chapter has a quite simple structure consisting of two levels: some remnants of an older account of a battle between the Israelites and a coalition of various groups under the king of Hazor, and a Deuteronomic reworking of the material's significance. The encounter takes place in northern Galilee near Merom, identified with the site of Meiron, presently under archaeological investigation.

In examining the chapter we can see in Joshua 11:1–15 an older stage prior to the D historian's overworking. Most of this older material represents a straightforward, uninterpreted presentation of the Israelites going out under Joshua to fight against the troops of their antagonists. A number of features characterize this older level. Although the resistance of the Canaanites and other peoples is frankly noted, this is balanced by the notion of the presence of Yahweh, who gives over the enemies into Israel's hands (vv. 6–9). There is no mention of the ban against the enemies and their possessions such as we have in verses 11–12 and 14. Rather, following the slaying of the king, Joshua is simply commanded to hamstring the horses and burn the chariots, both of which he does in obedience to the Lord's commands (v. 9). This same conflict is reflected in verse 10a, which records the attack against Hazor by the Israelites, once again part of the uninterpreted account.

It is probable, therefore, that the narrative up to this point is essentially an older nucleus which has been used by the D historian. Apparently among such northern tribes as Naphtali there survived traditions of battles which had taken place during the early period in this area. Joshua 11 is based on such accounts, and the traditions themselves may have stemmed from events on which recent excavations at Hazor may be able to shed some light. Here the destruction of the impressive Late Bronze Age city at the end of the thirteenth century B.C. has been attributed to the Israelites.[2]

It can be noted, however, that even this earlier material is overlaid with Deuteronomic additions or interpretations. The reference to Canaanites, Amorites, Hittites, Perizzites, Jebusites, and Hivites in Joshua 11:3 is just the sort of schematic listing familiar from Deuteronomy (Deut. 7:1; 20:17). The same holds for one of the strongest Deuteronomic ideas: the necessity of committing to the ban everything which belonged to the enemy. The force of this latter motif can be seen in Joshua 11:11–12 and 14–15, which are parallel to ordinances in the Deuteronomic style enunciated in Deuteronomy 7:2–6 and 20:16–18. What is noteworthy in Joshua 11:1–15, however, is the way in which older material is integrated by the D historian. In other instances throughout the work, ancient traditions are preserved in their earlier form which clearly collide with the D historian's own ideas. The theological implications of this fact, and their importance for a valid exegesis and interpretation of the D history, will be treated at several places below.

Nonetheless, it is characteristic of this historical work that the D historian's ideas come through with the greatest force. Such emphasis is evident in the remainder of the chapter in Joshua 11:16–23. This wrap-up of the conquest theme is clothed in Deuteronomic style, and the historian's theological judgments are exhibited. In his view, the most important aspect of the conquest of Joshua is not so much the wonder of taking the land, a point made elsewhere in his work, but the fact that Joshua obediently destroyed the enemy according to the requirements of the ban. According to the historian, Yahweh even strengthened the enthusiasm of the enemy to resist Israel, in order that the foe might more easily be eliminated (Josh. 11:20).

This narrative text gives one example of the way the D historian could use older materials in this work. Among such materials that he frequently uses are narrative accounts stemming from Israel's earlier historical traditions, tribal and boundary lists, saga cycles, annals, and a court history dealing with the reign of David and the problem of his successor. At two places the D historian even records a reference to older works being used. One of these was the Book of Jashar (Josh. 10:13; 2 Sam. 1:18); a second was the Book of the Acts of Solomon (1 Kings 11:41). So great is this wealth of material in the D history that the work may be described as an unusually compact historical work of the Old Testament. As a literary production it merits attention, and as an example of historiography in the ancient world it stands out in its distinctiveness.

THE D HISTORIAN'S THEOLOGY

Since this great amount of material was executed according to the distinctive viewpoint of the D historian, it will be useful at this point to state some basic ideas which appear at various places in his work. These notions are simply listed here. The way they are interwoven into the work will be seen in the sections considered below.

In the first place, Israel was viewed by the D historian as a chosen people, endowed with a special meaning in its history (Josh. 2:10; 1 Sam. 12:22; 1 Kings 8:16, 56, 57). This election consciousness permeates his work throughout. Second, the national or communal life of Israel was provided its identity through the laws and commandments attached to Israel's covenant (Deut. 5:1; 1 Kings 6:12–13). Third, for the D historian God was indivisible. This conviction of the oneness and unity of God had its counterpart in the idea of a single, unified people designated as "all Israel," a people which was to serve him with singular devotion of heart and soul (Deut. 6:4–5). In the fourth place, although the land was a pledge made much earlier to the fathers, by overcoming the people west of the Jordan Yahweh was seen to bring to fulfillment his promises, especially by means of the faithful work of Moses and Joshua (Josh. 11:10–23).

Fifth, related to the theme of Yahweh's oneness was the concentration of worship at the site of Jerusalem and the centralization of cultic activities at the temple in that city (Deut. 12; 2 Kings 23:4–5). The Israelites were to do away with threatening and competing cults, especially those associated with the Canaanites. Sixth, the D historian held his own version of royal theology, in which the Davidic representative was seen as the principal guardian of the covenant and was charged to live according to Yahweh's commands and covenant (1 Kings 2:1–4; 2 Kings 22:11–13). And finally, throughout his work the D historian viewed the history of Israel as one filled with urgency. In his view a choice was set before Israel, either to live in the commandments of Yahweh or to suffer the consequences of its rejection of them. Prophets were sent to warn her about her choice and her fate. Thus for the historian the prophets had special importance, and his work included traditions concerning the earlier prophets in particular.

AUTHOR AND DATE

A problem of importance arises concerning the identification of the author of the D history and the times in which he lived. Two viewpoints are possible. One is that the work is largely the product of a single individual. A second is that a school of closely associated traditionalists was responsible for the work and that it appeared in a number of stages. For the sake of simplicity we are using the designation D historian in this study, although that term could refer to a number of individuals if the reader would so prefer it.

Who this person was and what background he came from have

been widely discussed matters. On the basis of what has already been noted above, it would seem that he came from Jerusalem or nearby, and that he composed his work in this city. Here he had access to an abundance of materials which were used in his work. Some of the official court records with which he was familiar were deposited in the government buildings of this city. At the same time, an interesting feature is that the D historian also had knowledge of various traditions from north Israel. Again his access to these must have been in Jerusalem. It is probable that many of these northern traditions were collected and brought to the southern capital following the destruction of Samaria in 721 B.C.

The special interest the historian had in cultic matters suggests a close relation to the priestly classes, especially the Levites whom he seems to have favored (Deut. 12:12, 19; 18:1–8). Whether he himself was a priest, or a layman with close attachments to the priesthood, cannot be decided for certain. Nonetheless, we know that he viewed positively efforts on the part of the state administration to purify Israel's national life and to bring it into conformity with the covenant as he understood it. Two rulers especially were singled out as having made worthy contributions in this way, Hezekiah (2 Kings 18:3) and Josiah (2 Kings 22:2).

Since the D historian seems to have had such evident associations with the reform of the latter king, it has long been proposed that the Book of Deuteronomy was the core of the document found by Hilkiah the priest during Josiah's reign (2 Kings 22:8), and which thus spurred the movement to reform. The matter is still debated but this explanation seems plausible. The D historian may have been stimulated to compose his work, in part at least, by the Josianic reform and its impact. In any case he entertained a supportive view toward this reform (2 Kings 23:1–20).

Still another impetus seems to have prompted the composition of his work. At various places it is evident that the catastrophe of the exile of the people of Judah is in the mind of the historian. These dark events took their toll, and their consequences are reflected in other exilic and postexilic literature. That the D historian was compiling his work under the shadow of these happenings provides a significant context for understanding his work.

When did the final compilation of the D history take place? Differences of opinion are found on this matter, but several explanations are possible. One is that the work was written in two phases. The first took place prior to the exile, possibly during the days of Josiah, and at this time the major parts of the work were completed. The second occurred during the exile when the brief ending in 2 Kings 25:27–30 was appended. An alternative explanation is that the major part of the work was produced in the postexilic period, but this view presents more serious problems than can be discussed here. The present study is based on the view that the work was in progress well before the troops of Nebuchadnezzar reached the gates of Jerusalem. Consequently the history reflects some of the confusion of this period. Further additions, such as those in 1 Kings 8:46–53 and 2 Kings 25:27–30, strongly suggest a final, postexilic redaction.

A chronological peg of importance for either view is the reference to the freeing of Jehoiachin, the captive king of Judah (2 Kings 25:27). Since this event took place during the reign of Evil-merodach (Awil-Marduk) of Babylon in 561 B.C., this may be taken as the date by which time either the entire composition was completed, or during which the final redactions were made to an earlier work. We shall see how the socio-political dynamics immediately preceding the exile, as well as the exilic period itself, played an important part in the way the D historian formulated his presentation of the history of Israel.

CHAPTER TWO

THE STRUCTURE OF THE D HISTORY

Leaving the Book of Deuteronomy aside, although it is the introductory section to the work of the D historian, we can trace in Joshua through Kings the direction his interests have led him, the way he has organized his material, and the purpose behind his great literary work.

THE BOOK OF JOSHUA

In composing the part of the D history called later "the Book of Joshua," the D historian had an array of materials at his disposal. He laid out these sources in the form of a continuous narrative in which older materials were spliced together by shorter Deuteronomic comments and were sometimes relieved and enlivened by lengthier speeches supplied by the D historian himself. Whether an outline such as the following was in his mind or not is a moot question, but it does seem the material of the Book of Joshua breaks up into several divisions. First are the accounts of the preparations for and the actual crossing into the land west of the Jordan (Josh. 1—5). This is followed by an account which can be designated the "conquest tradition" (Josh. 6—11). Thereafter we find a series of chapters consisting of lists (Josh. 12—21) which register the different portions west of the Jordan taken as an "inheritance" by the tribes. Joshua 22 still belongs to this basic interest but deals with a special problem among the Transjordan tribes. In the final two chapters (Josh. 23—24) are a Deuteronomic farewell speech and an account of an early assembly of the tribal representatives at Shechem.

The D historian begins his work with his own ideas of Israel's crossing of the Jordan. These are couched in typical Deuteronomic speech. The initial speech in Joshua 1:1–9 is a reinforcement of the vocation of Joshua as the successor of Moses. It intimates the D historian's special interest in Joshua and the way in which he saw the latter's contribution to Israel's occupation of the land. The Deuteronomic interest in Joshua is found in Deuteronomy 1:38, as well as Joshua 3:7 and especially in the summing-up section which sees the time of Joshua as a period during which the people served Yahweh in an exemplary way (Josh. 24:31). Joshua's continuing speech at 1:10–18 is a call to preparation and an encouragement for the participation of the Transjordanian tribes of Reuben, Gad, and the half-tribe of Manasseh.

While Israel prepares to enter the land, the story of the spies and Rahab in Joshua 2 is introduced. This story is made up of an older account which the D historian has taken over mostly in its ancient form. At one point some parts of the account may have been transmitted orally, judging from the discordances in the narrative. The contrast in style between this older material and the sections supplied by the D historian is quite noticeable. The reference to Sihon and Og in Joshua 2:10b may reflect the editor's hand. The story of Rahab points to an explanatory or etiological interest in the problem of the family of Rahab the harlot and how it survived to live on among the Israelites at a later time.

Joshua 3 and 4 are heavily reworked chapters, containing the account of the crossing into the land and the setting up of groups of commemorative stones. Earlier levels of these two chapters' literary history show two apparent versions of the stone groups, one associated with the river and a second with the important site of Gilgal, whose exact location has yet to be established. With the latter site an old tradition of mass circumcision had come to be associated. This tradition was again reworked by the D historian (5:4).

The conquest theme properly begins with the saga of Jericho's demise in Joshua 6, an intriguing chapter with a complex literary form. Little modification by the D historian is evident in this chapter, as is also the case in the account of the sin of Achan and his family in chapter 7. Naturally the D historian found this case of the punishment of Achan's family for failing to carry out the law suitable to his own view.

From Jericho the Israelites advance into the hill country, where the story of the first phase of their acquisition of land unfolds (Josh. 8—9). Joshua 8 is the record of the attack against Ai, near Bethel. The D historian's editing can be seen in 8:1–2, and in the story of the construction of the altar on Mount Ebal in 8:30–35 (see Deut. 27:4–5). The episode of the Gibeonites who became hewers of wood and drawers of water for the altar on behalf of the Israelites (Josh. 9) is probably again an explanatory story (etiology) whose intent was to clarify how these non-Israelites had attached themselves to the Israelite community and its cult. The D historian's hand can be seen in 9:9–10, 24–25.

Joshua 10 introduces the second phase of the conquest, the drive against the five-king coalition in the southwest of the land, including Jerusalem and Hebron. Several older traditions have been molded together in this chapter. The D historian's hand can be seen in 10:9–10 and in his summation in 10:40–43. Joshua 11 is the account of the third and final phase of the conquest, telling of the battles in the north, which came to a successful climax chiefly against Jabin, king of Hazor. We have already noted in the first chapter how Joshua 11 contains older traditions edited by the D historian in 11:11–12, and of the historian's own final summary of the conquest in 11:16–23.

Joshua 12, although a list, is still attached to the conquest tradition. The list presents the towns taken, along with their kings or chieftains. Little if any Deuteronomic editing is present. The roster, especially the section of it in 12:7–24, contains some problems in that several towns listed elsewhere as having remained under Canaanite control (Judg. 1:27–33) are here recorded as having fallen in defeat before the Israelites.

Beginning with Joshua 13 and continuing through Joshua 21 a somewhat complex collection is found. These chapters are largely lists or accounts of the apportionment and settlement of the land east and west of the Jordan. The data recorded in these chapters are not unamimous in their details, and the divergences in the lists suggest stages in the settlement of the land by different groups attached to the later Israel. That such lesser clan or tribal groups as the Machirites in Transjordan (13:31), or the family of Caleb (14:6–15) were given special allotments, may reflect an older stage prior to the twelve-tribe system of Israel. The recognition of Joseph as a single tribe, while the same tribe was viewed as made up of Ephraim and Manasseh at a later stage (17:14–18), is also significant. Generally speaking, Joshua 13—21 comprises two basic types of lists which have been intermixed. One is a description of the boundaries of the tribal lands (boundary list) found in 13:8—14:5; 15:1–19; 16:1—18:20; 19:1–51. A second is a city list found in 15:20–63; 18:21–28, including a list of cities of refuge and the Levitical cities in chapters 20—21. Scholarship inclines toward seeing the boundary lists as having originated perhaps as late as the times of Josiah (640–609 B.C.). The D historian's comments are introduced at various points, such as in 13:14 and 21:43–45, as well as in the formulation of Caleb's request to Joshua in 14:6–15.

The account in Joshua 22 of the altar built in Transjordan by the tribes of Reuben, Gad, and the half-tribe of Manasseh is particularly instructive for the D historian's point of view. The chapter is heavily marked by Deuteronomic features, and the aim of the account, even though it turns out to have a positive ending, is to admonish against setting up a cult place in competition with the centralized one at Jerusalem.

We have already noted the importance of speeches at the turning points of history as the D historian viewed these. Such turning points would occur when an important person as Moses or Joshua moved close to death, or when particularly important events, such as the request for a king (1 Sam. 8), or the dedication of the temple (1 Kings 8) took place. At such points the D historian found it appropriate to introduce "speeches" fitting the importance of the moment. Usually these are presented in his characteristic style. Joshua 23 represents one of these. It is a final admonition of the aging leader, Joshua, stressing the responsibility of Israel.

Joshua 24 is a chapter of unusual importance, having played a significant role concerning the covenant formulas of Israel, discussed in Chapter Four. Verses 1–28 contain several seemingly older traditions, some of which may have been used as a cultic recitation. The Book of Joshua draws to a conclusion with burial traditions about Joshua (24:29–31), Joseph (v. 32), and Eleazar (v. 33).

THE BOOK OF JUDGES

The Book of Judges divides easily into four main sections as follows. Judges 1:1—2:5 is an account of the entry of the Israelites into the land of Canaan, different from that found in the Book of Joshua. Following this account, 2:6—3:6 is a Deuteronomic contribution serving as an introduction to the period treated in the book. The bulk of the book in 3:7 to 16:31 is united around the theme of Israel's deliverers or "the judges," although the material is diverse. Finally, Judges 17—21 is a series of appendixes, consisting of narratives regarding several tribal events.

The Book of Judges begins in a curious way with a tabulation of events which derive from an entirely different tradition of the conquest than that found in Joshua 1—11. This divergence has given rise to a large scholarly discussion. The question is whether the Book of Joshua is closer to the actual situation as the Hebrews began to take over the land, or whether Judges 1 reflects a more realistic appraisal. According to the latter there were many parts of the land which remained under Canaanite domination until a later time (1:27–33). Two points may be made but neither can be taken as conclusively proven. First, the narrative in Judges 1 appears to be an older account and for this reason may reflect a description nearer to the course of events. In that case the Book of Joshua may suggest considerable idealizing of what it records. Second, the archaeological evidence from some of the sites named tends to support the description in Judges 1. For example, it seems probable that Taanach and Megiddo remained Canaanite during the period of the judges, and were only later, at the time of David, introduced into Israelite control. Thus Judges 1:27 seems to be more accurate than Joshua 12:21 (see Josh. 17:11–12). In any case, Judges 1 betrays few Deuteronomic features outside the introductory formula at 1:1. At some point, the unique tradition of this chapter stressed the special role of the tribe of Judah in the movement into the land.

Judges 2:1–5 is a distinctive unit. Whether it shows signs of the D historian's reworking or not has been debated, but it seems likely that it does not.[3] The point of this account of a gathering of "all Israel" before the messenger at Bochim (=Bethel) is to stress the need to resist Canaanite influences. Altars were to be torn down as a sign of putting the covenant into practice. The language and description do not appear to be Deuteronomic, apart from a word or two, but it is easy to see that this thinking would lend itself to the D historian's basic understanding.

The large Deuteronomic introduction to the book in 2:6—3:6 is an important link in the D history. It serves to connect Joshua's speech and demise in Joshua 23 with the new period of the judges. The D historian's interpretation of Israel's past is clear: a recurrent cycle of obedience and blessing, giving way to apostasy and punishment, and followed again by the raising up of a judge under whom blessing and obedience would return once more. The last part of the unit records the nations whom Yahweh used to test Israel.

The main portion of the Book of Judges in 3:7—16:31 consists of two types of material which are used at great length by the D historian and into which he frequently introduces his own transitional remarks and summations. The first type consists of stories concerning a number of Israel's heroic "judges" or deliverers, such as Deborah, Gideon, and Samson. The second type is quite different, being a list of "minor judges" who were active in the early affairs of Israel and about whom little information survived, except for rather brief notices. The D historian has apparently constructed his own order of the succession of the judges, making use of both the judge lists and lengthier stories about several of Israel's deliverers. We cannot be sure that his sequence accurately reflects the course of history. In some cases two of the figures could have functioned at the same time, while the notation about Shamgar (3:31) is found in some manuscripts after the story of Samson (16:31). The two types of material may be seen as follows:

Longer Stories		*Brief Notices*	
Ehud	3:12–30	Tola	10:1–2
Deborah and Barak	4—5	Jair	10:3–5
Abimelech	9	Ibzan	12:8–10
Jephthah	10:6—12:7	Elon	12:11–12
Samson	13—16	Abdon	12:13–15

Among these various figures the group of five—Tola, Jair, Ibzan, Elon and Abdon—are described similarly (10:1–5; 12:8–15). Each of these is referred to as judging Israel, while exploits of saving Israel are not noted. This has given rise to the question whether these so-called minor judges may not have played somewhat different roles from the others who are usually mentioned as rising up to deliver Israel in a time of crisis. It is possible that the brief list of minor judges may reflect more specifically the term judge, and that they may have been in charge of dispensing justice under the system of tribal law developed in the period of the settlement. At the same time, the heroic stories may reflect a period when the judges had a larger role, involving not only juridical aspects, but also ruling and directing the military plans of the people and carrying out high-level decisions.

Within this complex of material a number of points may be observed. After beginning with brief descriptions of Othniel who delivered Israel from Cushanrishathaim, king of Mesopotamia, of Ehud who struck down Eglon, king of Moab, and of Shamgar who killed six hundred Philistines and delivered Israel, the story of Deborah and Barak is introduced. This account is found in both a prose (chap. 4) and a poetic version (chap. 5). It has long been noted that the two versions are not identical, and that the prose account contains items not found in the poetic version and vice-versa. Judges 4, for example, introduces Jabin, king of Hazor, into the story (Judg. 4:2; Josh. 11:1), while in Judges 5 it is Sisera who is the primary foe of Israel. On the other hand, both versions see the conflict culminating in the death of Sisera at the hands of Jael, who drives a peg through his temple or cheeks (Judg. 4:21; 5:24–26). Of the two versions, the poetic form in chapter 5 is probably the earlier, and indeed it bears the marks of Hebrew poetic style which scholars have dated not far from the probable time of the events recorded, about 1150 to 1125 B.C. Excavations conducted at Taanach (Judg. 5:19) have brought to light important Iron Age material which may bear upon the events lying behind these accounts.

The Gideon story (Judg. 6—8) is bracketed at both ends by Deuteronomic comments, which tie the older episodes to the larger history (6:1; 8:33–35). The narrative of Gideon contains a number of originally separate stories which have been gathered and presented in such a way as to supply a connected account. However, the seams joining these stories are sometimes thin, and their original independent status can be seen often. An example is the account of the tearing down of an altar of Baal, supposedly built by Gideon's father, Joash. The altar is said to have been torn down by Gideon, who was renamed Jerubbaal (6:25–32). It seems that a separate narrative dealing with Jerubbaal (cf. 9:1) somehow came to be attached to Gideon in composing the written tradition about the latter. How and why this episode was credited to Gideon is not clear, but the narrative as we now have it undertakes several attempts at harmonizing (7:1; 8:29). The basic story of Gideon, however, is of his call to serve as a deliverer, leading Israel in a military attack against its enemies, the Midianites and Amalekites. His success in routing them is seen by the D historian as one of the periods of salvation (8:35).

Much of the story of Abimelech and his abortive efforts to rule over Shechem as a king (chap. 9) derives from older sources. Beginning with his own remark in 13:1, the D historian introduces the cycle of stories about Samson in chapters 13—16. This entire cycle is noteworthy for its absence of Deuteronomic comments. The stories are included in their earlier form without interpretation. They depict Samson's birth (chap. 13), his marriage to a Philistine woman (chap. 14), remembered acts of vengeance against the Philistines (chap. 15), and his final activity at Gaza, including the story of Samson and Delilah (chap. 16). The stories no doubt reflect the conflicts of the tribe of Dan with the Philistines prior to its migration north (chap. 18), although much of the story of Samson would fit the category of folk story more than actual historical account. Its relation to the interests of the D historian is found in such places as 14:19, where the spirit of the Lord comes mightily upon Samson as it had upon other judges (see 11:29).

The final part of the Book of Judges consists of several supplementary stories dealing with the tribe of Dan and its migration to the north (chaps. 17—18) and the tribe of Benjamin during this period (chaps. 19—21). Very little Deuteronomic commentary is found in these chapters, outside the notation that there was no king in the land during these times (18:1; 19:1; 21:25). The latter point was one in which the D historian was interested insofar as he could view the kingship in retrospect as something that could have worked out as a promising possibility for Israel but which failed. The migration of

Dan to Laish in the far north of the country (18:27) suggests increasing pressures in the lowland country from such peoples as the Philistines. The image of Micah taken by the Danites and set up at Dan is an early reflection of the importance that this site achieved later as a cult center (1 Kings 12:29). The episode about the Benjaminites revolves around a crime committed by the men of Gibeah (Judg. 19:22–25). This story has many resemblances to the story of the sin of Sodom in Genesis 19:5. It reflects the turmoil of intertribal relations which occurred during this period, as well as the way in which the early tribes organized themselves to deal with it.

THE BOOKS OF SAMUEL

For the D historian the period of the judges continued into the times of Samuel. With the appearance of this many-colored personality on the scene, a new period was seen to be drawing near. The story of Samuel thus links up with what had preceded in the Book of Judges, while at the same time it anticipates the establishment of the new order of the monarchy. This transitional character of the period of Samuel is a marked feature of the first part of these books. The two books of Samuel divide easily into the following blocks of material: 1) Samuel's birth and call (1:1—4:1a), 2) the Ark Narrative (4:1b—7:1), 3) Samuel and Saul (7:2—15:35), 4) Saul and David (16:1—2 Sam. 1:27), 5) David as king (2 Sam. 2—8), 6) the Succession Narrative (2 Sam. 9—20; 1 Kings 1—2), and 7) several appendixes dealing with David's reign (2 Sam. 21—24).

Once again it can be seen that the D historian had at his disposal a diversity of material which he organized and to which he sometimes supplied his own interpretation. Among his material were old accounts about Samuel and Saul, a special history of the sacred ark, and a remarkable document concerned with the troubles of David's reign and the struggles involved in finding a successor. The D historian left no doubt as to how he saw this material contributing to his synthetic presentation. At several strategic places his notations can be seen in the form of explanatory transitions or longer speeches.

The old Samuel story lying behind 1 Samuel 1—3 contained a birth account and a report of Samuel's call through his close association with Eli. Since the crux of the story seems to have been the word "ask" (1:20), which is the meaning of the Hebrew name Saul, some have proposed that the story here attributed to Samuel's birth may earlier have been connected with Saul. There is no certainty on this matter, but the type of story found in 1 Samuel 1 was popular. It emphasized barrenness and the manner in which God could respond to a less than promising situation, bringing about the appearance of an important actor in his divine work. The Deuteronomic markings are minimal in this section, but 1 Samuel 2:35–36 may indicate his thoughts on the collapse of the Elide priesthood which in the course of the book is superseded by that of Zadok (2 Sam. 8:17; 15:24).

The narrative concerned with the ark in 1 Samuel 4:1b—7:1 traces the fortunes of this sacred object in early Israel from its capture by the Philistines at Ebenezer to its eventual disposition in the house of Abinadab at Kiriath-Jearim. This old ark history is resumed in 2 Samuel 6 when David brings the holy object to Jerusalem. There are no traces of D imprinting upon the story of the ark, and apparently the historian found it a suitable account in its own form to incorporate at these points.

Following the Ark Narrative, Samuel is once more introduced in 1 Samuel 7:3, playing a key role in many of the reports from 7:3 to 15:35. This entire section is important for the material it contains regarding a major transformation of ancient Israel's structure: from tribal society under judges to that of the monarchy. A summation of Samuel's work as judge (1 Sam. 7:15–17) suggests that during his period the end of the one religio-political form occurred and the second took over.

The section in 7:3—15:35 contains two major interests around which a variety of material is collected. One is the selection of Saul as Israel's first king; a second concerns itself with events during the reign of Saul, including battles with the Philistines and Amalekites. Of special importance are the two versions of the investiture of Saul as king. In one of these versions (8:4–22; 10:17–27) the request of the people for a king, and the granting of a king, are seen as essentially negative since they symbolize the refusal to live under an order with God himself as king over Israel. This account contains many Deuteronomic ideas and either was largely composed by the D historian or was heavily adapted to his thought. The second account in 9:1—10:16 presupposes the kingship as a positive institution for the welfare of ancient Israel. For this reason it has sometimes been taken as the older of the two. The tension between these two views and their presence in a single book is one of the intriguing aspects of the Book of First Samuel. In addition to the above Deuteronomic elements, we can see other marks of the negative viewpoint in Samuel's farewell discourse in 1 Samuel 12, which again assumes quite broadly the theme of the disobedience of Israel. The continuity with the Book of Judges in the D history can be noted in various references in this speech, such as those concerning Sisera (12:9; cf. Judg. 4), Jerubbaal (12:11; cf. Judg. 7:1) and Jephthah (12:11; cf. Judg. 11).

In 1 Samuel 16—2 Samuel 1, the theme of the rejection of Saul as king picks up momentum and when combined with the introduction into this story of his most feared competitor, David, leads eventually to the tragic end of Saul's kingship. Particularly noteworthy in this section is the lack of distinctive Deuteronomic comments. Apparently the historian presented without interpretation traditions drawn from a number of sources about Saul and David. It seems that some of these had been reworked prior to their being used by the D historian, for there is a decided tendency to denigrate Saul throughout, while David is presented in a favorable light, sometimes to an extreme degree as in the comments in 1 Samuel 16:18.

The section falls into three parts: 1) the rise of David and the gradual development of an evil spirit in Saul, including the story of David's victory over Goliath (1 Sam. 16—18), 2) David in flight while Saul pursues him (1 Sam. 19—27), 3) the wars with the Philistines which provide the context for the demise of Saul (1 Sam. 28—2 Sam. 1). The location of these events is in the North, in the Valley of Jezreel (1 Sam. 29:1), and both Saul's and Jonathan's deaths take place in the fierce battle on Mount Gilboa (1 Sam. 31:8). The Saul story comes to a conclusion with one of the most moving of biblical poems, the lament of David over Saul and Jonathan in 2 Samuel 1:19–27, a piece commonly attributed directly to David.

The first collection having to do with David's kingship is found in 2 Samuel 2—8. It tells of David's being anointed king over Judah at

Hebron (2:1-4), of his early battles, and of his dealings with the house of Saul over which he is finally successful (2:5—4:12). After being made king of Israel and becoming the head of a united kingdom (5:1-5), he attacks Jerusalem and makes it his capital (5:6-25). The resumption of the ark theme is found in 6:1-15, relating this section to the same source as the Ark Narrative in 1 Samuel 4:1b—7:1. The ark is described as finally having found its resting place in Jerusalem. The oracle of the prophet Nathan given to David in 2 Samuel 7 is a section with particular relevance to the concept of kingship in the Old Testament. The oracle is clothed in formulations similar to those of the D historian, which intimates that it is probably a later composition. Its main interest is the eternal covenant with the dynasty of David. Finally, 2 Samuel 8 is a unique chapter, consisting of a summation of David's victories. It is clearly from the hand of an editor, possibly from the D historian himself, who recapitulated the military exploits of David.

A composition which has attracted much attention in more recent study is 2 Samuel 9:1—20:26. It is often referred to as the Court History of David or the Succession Narrative. Its subject matter deals with critical events during the reign of David. Included are insights concerning David's court, such as the treatment of the crippled grandson of Saul in 2 Samuel 9, the wars of David in chapters 10—12 (in the context of which appears the David and Bathsheba story), the family difficulties of the king in chapter 13, and the rebellions during David's reign, fomented at first by his own son Absalom (chaps. 14—20). The straightforward, unadapted character of this history caused students of ancient Near Eastern historiography to point to it as a model of critical and literary clairvoyance. The hand of the D historian is barely visible in most of this material, and it appears that he simply incorporated this great work which may have been produced by a creative person living in David's court. The history reaches beyond the times of David to the beginning of Solomon's reign in 1 Kings 1:1—2:46. Since the materials are all pointed in that direction, it appears that the court historian was interested in tracing how the Davidic royal heritage passed over into Solomon's hands only with great difficulty following David's death.

The final chapters, 21—24, are a collection of miscellaneous material dealing with the end of David's reign. It is possible they were added very late as an appendix. The poetry purported to have come from David in 22:2–51 and 23:1–7 is a duplicate of Psalm 18. Chapter 24 is especially important for its account of the threshing floor of Araunah in verses 18–25. It was on this site that the later Solomonic temple was constructed, and this description therefore must have had some special cultic significance for the history of Israel's most important sanctuary. Its importance for the historian, in whose thought the Jerusalem temple played such a formative role, is evident.

THE BOOKS OF KINGS

It is in the study of the books of Kings that the understanding of a single, comprehensive historical work composed by the D historian has special significance. Such a perspective provides a meaningful structure for what would otherwise seem to be a tedious listing of the kings of Judah and Israel along with limited data about their reigns. Seen as part of a continuous history unfolding under divine judgment and mercy, however, these books are provided an entirely new perspective. They also have unique significance because in them the D historian draws his work to a finale. Especially in regard to the Babylonian disaster, his material raises historical and theological questions of the greatest importance.

The books of Kings again contain a diversity of material. It is obvious from what the D historian notes many times in 1 and 2 Kings that he used sources for the history of the kings of Israel and Judah. These were no doubt written documents chronicling events of a particular king's reign. In one case a chronicle is noted as having to do with a single king, such as the "book of the acts of Solomon" (1 Kings 11:41). Elsewhere we find reference to the "Book of the Chronicles of the Kings of Israel" (1 Kings 14:19) and to the "Book of the Chronicles of the Kings of Judah" (1 Kings 14:29). The latter two are referred to often as a source. In addition the D historian had at his disposal traditions about important prophetic figures. Thus in 1 Kings 11 we find material on the prophet Ahijah; in chapters 17—21 there occurs a lengthy collection about Elijah; in chapter 22 Micaiah is sketched in a memorable account; and finally in 2 Kings 1—9 a cycle of stories concerning Elisha is interposed. Alongside this material we can observe a large number of the D historian's own remarks. In fact, the books of Kings contain a larger number of Deuteronomic speeches and transitional remarks than the books discussed previously.

The books of Kings fall easily into a number of sections. First is the continuation of the Succession Narrative in 1:1—2:46. This is followed by Solomon's reign in 1 Kings 3—11, and by a long composition dealing with the period between Rehoboam's reign and that of Ahaziah of Israel (chapters 12—22). In 2 Kings, the first part in chapters 1—17 deals with the period from Ahaziah of Israel to the end of the northern kingdom, while chapters 18—25 are devoted to the span of time between Hezekiah and Jehoiachin of Judah, that is, to the final days of the Judean state.

In our overview of the structure of this material we shall concentrate on noting the Deuteronomic elements in each section and the manner in which he tied sections together. The older blocks of material used by the D historian can be examined by the reader separately. The continuation of the Succession Document in 1 Kings 1—2 brings to a climax the struggle for David's throne, portraying the success over Adonijah achieved by Solomon and his supporters. The document ends with the D historian's statement that the kingdom was established in the hands of Solomon (2:46b). Among other Deuteronomic contributions is the charge from David to Solomon in 1 Kings 2:2–4, which is reminiscent of the transition of power from Moses to Joshua in Joshua 1:6–9 and Deuteronomy 31:23. Here the emphasis on obedience is clearly a strong feature of the D historian's understanding of the challenge continually laid before Israel's leaders. Still another D emphasis occurs at 1 Kings 2:27, which sees the death of Abiathar as a fulfillment of the prophecy against the house of Eli (see 1 Sam. 3:11–14). The D historian's own material appears at key points. His theology of the central importance of Jerusalem shines through in the mildly apologetic statement in 1 Kings 3:2, that the reason the people sacrificed formerly at high places was because there was as yet no centralized sanctuary.

It is not surprising that in connection with the building of the temple we find some of the expanded Deuteronomic formulations.

Much more extensive is the interesting prayer for the dedication of the temple in 1 Kings 8:23–61, which exhibits cardinal elements of the historian's theology. The final summing up of Solomon's reign, as the D historian assessed it, contains judgments about his role for the future of Israel. In 1 Kings 11:2, 4–8 and 11–13, Solomon's numerous marriages with foreign women are singled out for causing the drifting away from the covenant. In all, the D historian could not finally conclude that Solomon's reign was a positive period in the history of Israel.

The tragic division of the kingdom which occurred soon after the death of Solomon was understood by the D historian as a punishment against the Solomonic household for its failure to do away with the competing cults of Ashtoreth and other deities, and for its failure to follow the commandments and statutes of the old covenant. All of the words belonging to the speech of Ahijah to Jeroboam in 1 Kings 11:31–39 are strongly shaped by the historian's own formulations. The rebellion of the ten northern tribes is seen, along with the end of the northern and southern kingdoms, as an event with special significance in the judgment against the evil period of the kings.

An especially important chapter for gaining insight into the D historian's way of handling his data and historical views is 1 Kings 13. Its theme is the condemnation of Jeroboam I, who introduced into Israel the sanctuaries of Dan and Bethel (1 Kings 12:29). Chapter 13 contains the account of the opposition of several prophets to Jeroboam's activity and reign. The hand of the D historian can again be seen in several of his typical formulas in such places as 1 Kings 13:2. The verse reads back into this earlier period the name of Josiah, the king of Judah to receive greatest acknowledgment from the D historian. The allusion here to Josiah's burning the bones at Bethel is taken up again in 2 Kings 23:16–18. In 1 Kings 13 the D historian is writing out of the events of the reign of Josiah during the late seventh century B.C.

As the D historian proceeds, beginning with the materials in 1 Kings 14, we find him interweaving materials from the king lists of Israel and Judah. The synchronisms found in these accounts have been studied for their chronological value during the period of the divided monarchy. It is not necessary to detail here what can be found in the commentaries and introductions to the books of Kings. What is more useful is to continue to focus attention on the D historian's framework for this material. Thus we can note that the account of Rehoboam's failures as outlined in 14:22–24 is expressed in a typical Deuteronomic formulation. His successor, Abijam, is similarly singled out for walking as did his father with a heart not wholly obedient (15:3–5). However, here the D historian notes his own belief that the dynasty was not cut off, both because of the earlier promises given to David and because David had indeed been a righteous king, except for his sin against Uriah.

Following Abijam, Asa is assessed as a king who performed certain acts according to the Davidic ideal. He removed male prostitutes in the cult along with the idols, but he failed to act similarly against the high places (15:11–15). As for the North, both Nadab (15:26) and Baasha (15:34) are noted for walking in the evil way of Jeroboam. Other northern kings against whom a similar judgment is made are Elah (16:13), Zimri (16:19), Omri (16:25–26), Ahab (16:30–34), and Ahaziah (22:51–53). Of the Judean king, Jehoshaphat, it is noted that he did effect certain positive changes, but again he retained the high places (22:43). All these judgments are stated in the form of Deuteronomic formulas.

As an example of the large blocks of material the D historian could introduce at some points, we find in 1 Kings 17:1—22:38 a collection dealing with Elijah and Ahab, Ahab's wars against the Syrians, the story of Naboth's vineyard, and the account of Jehoshaphat and the prophet Micaiah. Some of this material, such as the Elijah stories, must have originated in a different collection, while other material seems to have been taken from some of the chronicles used by the historian. It is notable that none of the data are worked over by the D historian, and throughout these chapters identifiable Deuteronomic characteristics are virtually absent.

The same situation prevails in the case of the traditions dealing with Elisha the Tishbite in 2 Kings 1—9. Most of the material in these chapters derives from an Elisha cycle of stories, although it is interspersed with historical accounts, probably again taken from the chronicles. Only at several points do we find the D historian's comments, in 3:2–3 and 8:27. The first is a typical Deuteronomic judgment of Jehoram of Israel; the second, a condemning assessment of Ahaziah of Judah.

The strong action by Elijah against the prophets of Baal is continued by Jehu, king of Israel. The D historian makes some positive comments about him at the same time that he recognizes that he did not carry out a total reform (2 Kings 10:28–31). During the same period Athaliah, the queen mother in Jerusalem, managed to take over the throne for a short period, destroying all members of the royal family except Joash. With the support of Jehoida the priest, Joash (Jehoash) ultimately succeeded to the throne. The historian acknowledges the latter's reign as one during which he did what was right, with the exception that he allowed the high places to continue (2 Kings 12:2–3).

Two Israelite kings are introduced following Jehu, and both are noted as having done evil by following in the ways of Jeroboam I. Jehoahaz is mentioned in 2 Kings 13:2–3 and Jehoash (son of Jehoahaz) in 13:11. Corresponding to the same period is Amaziah who is judged, like other Judean kings, as having done certain things in accordance with the D historian's conception, but who also failed to raze the high places (14:3–4). Following this correlation of the rulers of the two kingdoms, King Jeroboam II, well known from the times of Amos and Hosea, is cited as coming to the throne in the North. The historian notes the preference this king had for the sins of his namesake (14:24), even though he is also seen as having done much good for Israel. In Judah the new king Azariah (Uzziah) is rated as one who in part did what was right but again left the high places untouched (15:3–4).

The main interest of chapters 15—17 centers on the last years of the northern kingdom and its capital at Samaria, before its dissolution under Shalmanezer V (17:6) and Sargon II, who completed the destruction (Isa. 20:1). The last kings of Israel, with the exception of Shallum, are each assessed similarly by the D historian as having done evil. These include Zechariah (15:9), Menahem (15:18), Pekahiah (15:24), and Pekah (15:28). Alongside these, the southern king, Ahaz, is also appraised as one who failed to meet the standards predicated by the D historian (16:2–4). The last king of

Israel, under whom the disaster occurs, was Hoshea, again noted for his failure (17:2). In connection with the latter's reign, and along with earlier source material for the historical catastrophe of the northern kingdom, the D historian in 2 Kings 17 introduces a lengthy interpretation of his views on why Israel was led inevitably to these dark days. The chapter is an extensive Deuteronomic contribution.

Hezekiah's reign over Judah is told at some length in 2 Kings 18–20. The D historian begins the account by assessing positively the role of this king (18:3). There follow lengthy segments of pre-deuteronomic material, paralleled at Isaiah 36—39. The hand of the historian is evident in his description of Israel's sin (18:12) and in the prayers at 19:15–19 and 20:2–6.

Hezekiah is succeeded by Manasseh, who is assessed negatively in 21:2–16. This entire section is from the D historian, and the catalogue of grievances against Manasseh, in addition to the threats associated with his evil reign, show that for the historian Manasseh was particularly responsible for the movement of events toward Judah's final catastrophe. It was Manasseh who seduced the people of Judah to more and more evil and who thus opened the way to the ineluctable, divine judgment. Following Manasseh the reign of Amon is noted as introducing no improvement over his father's reign before him (21:20–22).

For the D historian, the period of Josiah had determinative significance. The account of this king's reign is found in 22:1—23:30. Only this king, besides David and Hezekiah, is given a full stamp of approval (22:2), even though his actions were not seen to be sufficient to reverse the evil set in motion by Manasseh (23:26–27). Although the account of Josiah's reign is based on sources available to the historian, the entire episode was heavily worked over by the D historian's interpretation of the events. The "book of the law" found by Hilkiah in the temple (22:8) has provided the basis for understanding the whole D history as being an expression of the dynamics at work during Josiah's reform. Whether it actually provoked the reform, however, is a disputed matter. The period was a high point for the historian, and his own participation in the events was probably considerable.

After Josiah's reign the D history moves quickly toward its conclusion. Jehoahaz is presented briefly as an evil king (23:32), as is also his successor, Jehoiakim, who was established as king over Judah by the Egyptians (23:37). The final days of Judah are recounted in 2 Kings 24—25, along with the last two kings of the south, Jehoiachin and Zedekiah. Both men are reckoned along with the evil kings of Judah (24:9, 19). Perhaps the last clear Deuteronomic assertion is found in 24:3–4, a statement which underscores his basic contention that Judah's destruction was a judgment of God directed toward the long history of disobedience, and specifically to the evil committed by Manasseh.

The history concludes with the events of the captivity of Jerusalem (25:8), and the conditions which followed in the wake of Nebuchadnezzar's attack on this city. The ending of 2 Kings (25:27–30) presupposes a gap of some years during the exile itself before Jehoiachin was set free from his arrest in Babylon. For this reason, it may be that these final verses were appended to the book to update the final outcome of the destruction so carefully sketched by the D historian.

Thus, in the D history from Joshua through 2 Kings, we find an elaborately constructed presentation, beginning with the end of Moses' leadership of the tribes in Transjordan down through the period of the settlement and monarchy to the end of the two kingdoms. Few figures from the past have left us a portrayal on any subject made with such intensity as has this compiler, thinker, and writer. It is in order for us to look more closely at some of the central ideas and concepts which were at the heart of his presentation.

CHAPTER THREE

PEOPLEHOOD

A dynamic concept which underlies the D historian's comprehensive work was his idea of Israel as a people. The questions of who Israel was, where she had come from, the unique basis for her solidarity as a people, and her special character, are presupposed throughout by the historian as problems of great importance. International events adapted from chronicles and annals might have interested him, but only to the extent that they could cast light upon his people's calling. The historical work from Joshua through Kings is thus a highly theological work, motivated by an interest in the deepest questions affecting Israel's self-understanding.

The basis for the D historian's concept of peoplehood lay in older ideas which he had taken over. Particularly formative for his ideas were the traditions of covenant ceremonies in which the ancient tribes were described as having been bound together into a single community before Yahweh. Thus the ceremony at Shechem in Joshua 24 above all had a special significance for him. In this account, the tribes were recollected as having come together at a particular moment, and from this gathering a new community took shape, a united people called Israel. That unity rested in the choice to abandon the tribal deities to which some of the various groups may once have given allegiance and to acknowledge Yahweh alone as the object of adoration and obedience. Whether the notion of a single commitment to a single God was in reality as complete and perfect as the historian later envisioned it, he could not fail to look back at this earlier period as an ideal one. Joshua especially was seen as having played a strong role in forging the unity of the people at this time, and thus Joshua was viewed by the historian with approval (Judg. 2:7).

In order to understand how the D historian conceived of the people of Israel, it is necessary to recall the circumstances under which he was writing. These were the events of the Babylonian conquest and the destruction of Jerusalem. Accompanying these events was a widespread, public sense of loss and defeat over the termination of the Davidic dynasty ruling over Jerusalem and Judah, the destruction of the temple itself, and the end of independent governance of the land. Following from these events there arose a crisis in the concept of who Israel was, and what she was meant to be. Thus we find in the D history a reflex of the self-searching of this era, an interest in defining Israel's sense of peoplehood which sprang from the agonizing concerns of the time.

The D historian reached to past traditions, not just to provide a historical sketch of who Israel was, but to discover roots and causes which could help to explain the tragedy surrounding her. Moreover, it seems that the concept of Israel which operated throughout his work, was more an ideal of what Israel ought to have been rather than what she had been in fact. This statement needs to be balanced by the observation that the D historian did see some periods, such as those of Joshua or David, as times which had come very close to concretizing the ideal. But it holds nevertheless that his judgment of the real Israel was in the light of an image of a more perfect Israel which he carried in his mind.

According to this ideal, Israel was a unique people gathered in committed unity under the divine commandments and statutes. This is the understanding of Israel for which a theoretical basis is given in Deuteronomy 1—3. It is also assumed in Deuteronomy 6:4 in the $š^e ma^c$ ("Hear, O Israel"), which elaborates the oneness of God as the corollary and most distinctive basis for the constitution of Israel itself. The people's oneness and the singleness of its commitment are coextensive with the divine unity which the $š^e ma^c$ reveres. We can see how this picture of a unified Israel under the single covenant dominates the concept of the D history throughout.

An example of the way this concept shaped the historian's presentation can be observed in the way he handled the lengthy registers of tribal boundaries, as well as the later city lists in Joshua 13—21. This material is diverse, as we have seen, and it also projects a picture of the settlement of the Hebrews in Cisjordan which must have been quite complicated, reflecting various tribal movements into the area which could not have taken place all at once or in a short time. The historian presents this material without interjecting into it his own interpretations. Nevertheless, it is evident that what he meant to convey in structuring his history with this material at just this place was a particular view of Israel. In his view the people of Israel was a unity as far back as the period of the settlement in the land. His usage of Joshua 24 underscores this. As Israel began to enter the land it did so with a united strategy and with a blueprint of how this territory, once it had been taken from its enemies, was to be apportioned as individual inheritances to each of the tribes. There is again an implicit sense of the unity and singleness of the people, even in the way the older lists are used.

Once Israel was in the land the historian saw things happening to the united tribes under a single perspective. The account of events during the period of the judges is telescoped through the D historian's basic outlook, that Israel's history was a testing ground for her faithfulness or disobedience to God. He had little interest in understanding causes of events which might be other than theological ones. The historian looked at his data not as a modern historian would, attempting to let them speak for themselves. Rather he discerned in whatever happened to Israel in the early years of her existence the hand of God either saving or punishing her. All of her history was an unfolding drama, a succession of moments of success and prosperity followed by stretches of disappointment and failure. This pattern is fully discernible in the Book of Judges, where the historian's view is often set forth explicitly (Judg. 2:6–7, 11–23). That the historian could use repeatedly stock phrases such as "the people of Israel did what was evil in the sight of the Lord" or "they forsook the Lord," or "the anger of the Lord was kindled against them and he gave them over to their enemies," points to the unified outlook under which the variegated data of his sources were understood.

What we see in the Book of Judges continues into the history of the monarchy in the books of Samuel and Kings. We have seen that there may have been more than one individual involved in the presentation of the D history. But regardless of how this problem is resolved, the view is still strikingly similar in all of these books. Israel is one people under a single God, confronted by the perennial test of events in which she found herself. Each period within her history is judged by the historian for its success or failure in putting into effective practice the ideal of being the obedient Israel. Even with the political and social transformation which followed the change from tribal government to monarchy, the issues remained the same. And thus a continuity in viewpoint is found from Judges right on through the books of Samuel and Kings.

Careful attention to the language of the D historian brings out even more clearly this passion for a unified concept of Israel. Expressions which are featured throughout the D history, such as "all Israel," "all the people of Israel," "the whole congregation of the Lord," or simply "the people of Israel," show that from his perspective the people of Israel had come into being by a special act of divine choice already in the age of the fathers, because even at this time Yahweh had begun to make promises of land to the ancestors of Israel (Josh. 1:6). This choice of Israel was confirmed in the days of Moses and Joshua, as the Book of Deuteronomy asserts (Deut. 7:6; 14:2; 26:18). Thus Israel was singled out to be a special people set apart from other peoples. Its social and political institutions undergirded this idea of a theocratically established people, for even the king eventually was called to view his position as one full of responsibilities to the great congregation of Israel (1 Kings 8:15–53).

The true test of this notion of an ideal Israel, set apart in its uniqueness under the commandments of God, came in the encounter of Israel with the surrounding nations. For the D historian the period of the settlement in Cisjordan opened a new and dangerous chapter in the history of Israel. Precisely here there began that lengthy course of events so full of crises, in which Israel would be faced with deciding either to be obedient to her destiny, or to deny it and be plunged into confusion and sometimes hopelessness. Crises of this sort began to emerge already in the period of the Transjordan wanderings, as in the case of the temptation into which the people fell headlong at Baal-peor (Deut. 4:3; Num. 25:1–18). But they became especially serious when Israel encountered the advanced culture of Canaan. When this began to occur, Israel, fresh out of the wilderness, was seen as facing a new time of decision. Now the questions of Israel's own identity as a separate people, and the uniqueness of her God, presented themselves inescapably as the most urgent of all problems.

The central issue of Israel and the surrounding peoples opened up a variety of subsidiary, practical concerns. Important were not only the problems of adapting features of Canaanite agricultural-technological culture. It was also a pressing matter to decide on situations of smaller scale such as those of intermarriage. This issue, which seems to have demanded no disproportionate attention in the earlier traditions of Israel, became increasingly significant during the centuries in which a symbiosis between Israelite and Canaanite culture was taking place. The D historian's own view is projected back into the period of Joshua. In the farewell speech of Joshua, a piece which is largely elaborated by the D historian himself, we can see this viewpoint in his own words: "For if you turn back, and join the remnant of these nations left here among you, and make marriages with them, so that you marry their women and they yours, know assuredly that the Lord your God will not continue to drive out these nations before you" (Josh. 23:12–13a; cf. Deut. 7:3–4). Although we gain some perspective on the mentality operative here from a comparative study of taboos on exogamy, the distinctive feature of this admonition is that it is an element of a larger emphasis on the uniqueness of the people, their God, and the land which they are occupying. In other words, it is more than tribalistic idiosyncrasy which is being expressed here. The unique vocational awareness of Israel was at stake, a self-awareness which could easily be swept away by uncritical openness to a dominant Canaanite culture in the areas west of the Jordan.

At least this was the vantage point from which the D historian saw the matter. For him the idea of a set-apart (the meaning of "holy") people was essential, not only because the earliest covenant with God had made them such, but because this separateness was tied to the problem of self-definition. It became a matter of truth itself, and the gravitation of Israel toward intermixing with the peoples in the land could only result in the spoilage of her integrity. Two of her kings were notable for having done just this through their intermarriage with persons from among foreign peoples. One of these was the otherwise enviable Solomon, whose marriage to many different wives from the surrounding peoples resulted in his introducing such gods as Ashtoreth of the Sidonians and Milcom of the Ammonites into Israel (1 Kings 11:1–5). From the D historian's perspective he had failed to follow the command of the Lord in doing so. A second example was Ahab of Israel, whose marriage to Jezebel, the daughter of Ethbaal, king of the Sidonians, resulted in the further encroachment of the worship of Baal into Israel (1 Kings 16:31).

The "other peoples" are thus elevated to a theological level in the thinking of the historian. No longer are they simply peoples living in the land which Israel is settling. They are symbolically potent entities whose very existence poses a threat. They are extensions of destructive forces residing in the nature of the gods whom they worship and represent. When we compare some of the ostensibly older material in the D history with the historian's own interpretations, the difference of viewpoint becomes evident. So, for example, the straightforward, almost secular description of David's battles with the Ammonites and Syrians (2 Sam. 10:1–19) stands in significant contrast to the considerable theologizing the historian is usually prone to make when referring to the foreign peoples. For him the people in the land are to be "driven out," not simply to make room for those entering to take up their inheritance, but more seriously because the commingling of Israel with the peoples could only result in peril to the latter (Josh. 11:16–20).

It is in this connection that we must understand one of the most difficult aspects of the D historian's ideology, his ideas about the execution of the ban (*herem*). The D history abounds with a commitment to the ancient notion of the ban, and ideas which stem from it. The historian's fundamental position on this is stated in Deuteronomy 20:13–18. Ideally when Israel was to enter the land and to begin to take over its cities and territories, she was to destroy the males—taking the women, children, cattle, and everything else as booty. In the case of cities belonging to the Hittites, Amorites, Canaanites, Perizzites, Hivites and Jebusites, nothing whatsoever was to be left since it was these peoples who would teach Israel to sin against God.

This basic idea is important in the conquest narratives of Joshua

gists at key sites of the conquest tradition, such as at Lachish or
Hazor, should alert us to the fact that there may well have been
severe military encounters which occurred intermittently in the days
of the settlement. On the other hand, as far as the D historian is
concerned, we probably do well not to press the literal side of his
description. His story was employed as a concept rich for its sym-
bolic value for his audience. It was a way of setting before them as
decisively as he was able the gravity of their own religious and cultural crises, and the ways by which the latter had been generated.
For the present-day interpreter these descriptions need to be read in
the light of the author's concern for emphasizing Israel's separateness, rather than as a wholly accurate historical description of her
settlement of the land.

A modern interpreter of the D history will thus find some difficulties with which he/she must grapple in translating the message
of the historian into a word for a modern audience. Clearly a simple
application of the Book of Joshua to recent wars and their legitima-
tion is unacceptable. Efforts along this line have sometimes been
responsible for fostering attitudes which are untenable and even
dangerous. Elsewhere the D historian's ban-ideology has been used
as an endorsement for acts which were flagrantly genocidal. The
strong note of exclusivity throughout the work has also been employed
unfortunately to justify the rupture of genuine strivings for community and unity. This negative side of an approach to the D history
needs to be thought about carefully in respect to any application of
his notion of peoplehood. It should lead us to see that neither the
uncritical acceptance of the texts, on the one hand, nor bowdlerizing
them, on the other, is acceptable.

A realistic view should open these texts to us, and to hearing what
may be a legitimate word out of this great historical work in the present context. A religious community which exists in the framework of
a pluralist social structure, as most do today, will surely need to
engage itself with the transmission of its beliefs and values to succeeding generations. We will find a great deal of sympathy in the historian
for such questions. Although his solutions cannot be those of committed religious people in our own time, modern searchers will not
fail to learn much from the way in which the people's identity in its

life with Yahweh surfaces as a major issue at nearly every important point in the historian's work. Living as he did at a time when Israel confronted a new situation among the foreign nations and their gods, this problem became critical for him. Any contemporary group of religious people striving for a comparable authenticity will appreciate the struggles of his conscience and soul as he envisioned a role and destiny for his people.

CHAPTER FOUR

COVENANT

If Israel enjoyed a singular relationship to her God, it was because of the ancient covenant which more than anything else provided a special dimension for her national life. The concept of covenant was formative for the D historian's work, and even where it is not expressly referred to, it is basic to all his thinking about the nation of Israel. There are several different uses of the idea of covenant in the D history, as well as several underlying notions of covenant which stand in some tension with each other. Our purpose in this chapter will be to organize some of the material about covenant which is scattered throughout his work and to attempt an interpretation of his thoughts and his use of this important idea.

That the notion of covenant was basic to the D historian's understanding may be seen first of all by looking at the Book of Deuteronomy. Although this book does not belong to our area of investigation, it must at least be kept in mind as the basic theological platform for the historian's work. Modern scholarship has shown that the Book of Deuteronomy presupposes the pattern of what must have been an annual ceremony dedicated to the renewal of the covenant. This is a helpful hypothesis for explaining why so much covenant language is present in Deuteronomy. At such a ceremony certain formal activities were undertaken. The renowned deeds of God, which had established the basis for the covenant, were recollected. Then the responsibilities of the people were set forth in the form of commands, accompanied by homiletical exposition. The latter is so characteristic of the style of large parts of Deuteronomy that it is a very suggestive explanation.[4] It is even probable that this Deuteronomic type of recital and elaboration influenced psalms which recount the salvation history and the people's obligations in the face of it, such as Psalms 105 and 106. Other features pointing to the covenant would be the curse formulas in Deuteronomy 27, which make most sense if seen against the background of a ceremony of covenant reevaluation and recommitment.

These peculiar features of covenant in Deuteronomy have been much studied in recent years in the light of ancient Near Eastern treaty texts, which have striking resemblances to the formal elements of covenant making and renewal as perceived by Deuteronomy and even earlier in such places as Exodus 20 and 24. For the study of the D historian's work, however, the important starting place is Joshua 24, a chapter which contains several sections of unusual importance. The first portion of the chapter, verses 2–13, is a brief, historical recital which, because of its succinct and formalized language, has been viewed as a small liturgical piece. This part, it is assumed, expresses the memory of the salvation deeds performed by God, on the basis of which a covenant could be made, and it must have been at home in early Israel. In verses 14–18 there follows the challenge to the people to take up the relationship of the covenant, to break connections with their formerly revered gods and to worship only Yahweh. This exclusive worship they agree to do by voicing a formalized confession. A third element in verses 19–24 is a carefully constructed counterclaim that Israel would not serve the Lord, followed by the calling upon the people as witnesses against themselves. Finally, in verse 25 the covenant is concluded and is accompanied by ordinances and statutes, perhaps kept in some documented form at the sanctuary at Shechem.

If this interesting chapter does indeed reflect formal covenant-making rites which were at home in ancient Israel, then it shows how deeply the D history's fundamental ideology had grown out of the older traditions of Israel, just as in the case of his ideas about peoplehood. He is not entirely an innovator. He used older traditions on which to build his distinctive word for a people in the midst of new crises. Not only is Joshua 24 important as an old tradition of covenant making. This historian also maintained an interest in the site with which that chapter is associated. Thus he brings out elsewhere the importance of the Shechem region as the place where the early commands were given by Yahweh to Israel. In Deuteronomy 27:12–

13, the dual mountains flanking the Shechem pass, Ebal and Gerizim, are noted for the role they played in the old curses and blessings. That the historian could place this important material in the introductory book of his work shows how strongly the old Shechem based covenant played into his thinking.

This is similarly the case for the interest he had in the history of the ark incorporated in the form of an ancient account in 1 Samuel 4:1b—7:1 and 2 Samuel 6:1–15. The ark had a number of different meanings in ancient Israel: it was the place where the presence of God resided in a special way; it functioned as a palladium carried before Israel into battle. The D historian, however, preferred to view the ark as a repository of the covenant. According to the historian, Moses had already been instructed by Yahweh to put the two tablets into this sacred installation (Deut. 10:2). Accordingly, for the D historian the ark came to be known most prominently as the "ark of the covenant," whether he was responsible for this terminology or not. It is the "ark of the covenant" that is to be carried before the people as they cross the Jordan (Josh. 3:6) and as they encircle the city of Jericho (Josh. 6:6). Again it is the "ark of the covenant" for which Solomon had built the temple and which he was to bring up to Jerusalem in one of the most patently Deuteronomic sections (1 Kings 8:1). In contrast to this idea of the ark is the old ark history incorporated by the historian in 1 Samuel 4:1b—7:1 and 2 Samuel 6:1–15, where the term used consistently for this sacred object is the "ark of God." Once again fundamental for the D historian is the idea that Israel is the people of the covenant.

A further example of what may be an older covenant tradition assimilated into the D history is the Bochim incident in Judges 2:1–5. Scholars have debated whether this brief description has been overworked by the historian, or whether it belongs to an earlier level of the tradition. In our opinion the unit does not reflect the dominant Deuteronomic mentality in either style or content, although it could well have come from circles to which the D historian was related. On one side, it expresses ideas which were fundamental for the historian, such as the command to break down the altars (Judg. 2:2). Yet these are not expressed in the style typical of the historian. However, regardless of how this problem is solved, the chief notion in this unit is that of the covenant and the conditions attached to it. Four elements are important for the way the brief narrative is structured. First is the assertion of the exodus as the grounds for a covenant with his people which Yahweh would never break (Judg. 2:1). Second is the command to the people to make no covenant with local inhabitants and to tear down their altars (Judg. 2:2a). This is followed, thirdly, by the provocation that they have not obeyed, formalized into the question "What is this you have done?" (Judg. 2:2b; cf. Gen. 3:13). And lastly is the terse speech of God, which is actually an elementary curse formula dealing with the announcement of impending punishment (Judg. 2:3).

As in the case of Joshua 24, this small text seems to reflect older notions of the covenant which were to have an impact on the historian. If earlier patterns of covenant making contained such elements as recital of the relation between the covenanting parties, stipulations, witnesses, deposition of the covenant document, and threat or welfare implicit in the curses and blessings, then we can see some of these basic elements in this unit. We can also understand how the Bochim tradition could catalyze the historian's perceptions of the meaning of the covenant in the crises of his own time. For him the entire history of Israel from Moses to the present is only understandable when seen in the pattern of the covenant and its different parts. The divine grace which established Israel is typically assumed as the point of departure, but equally important are the responsibilities of Israel herself as an actor in the relationship. So important is this element of accountability that all of Israel's history is lived out as though it were before witnesses (Josh. 24:27). By means of this view Israel has come to know terrible adversity, not because of the unpredictable course of history, but because of her great, collective offense against the expectations which the covenant sets before her. This encompassing view of the national history from a covenant perspective can be seen most clearly in the D historian's elaborate summary in 2 Kings 17:7–41.

Thus far, we have been looking at ways by which the historian builds his own conceptions of the covenant on older notions. Now it is important to look more closely at the several types of covenant which had come to play such an important part in Israel's self-understanding and the preferences of the D historian in regard to the differing types. This is a significant problem because it will help to put us in touch with some of the D historian's own basic theological concerns. As we look at several of the traditional covenant types with which he works, we shall ask whether he felt any suspension or even dichotomies between them, whether he preferred one particular type of covenant over another, or whether they tended to stand side by side in apparently unresolved tension in his work.

We can clear out of the way at the outset some instances of covenant in the D history which are not central, although they may illustrate the notion of covenant in the ancient Near Eastern human and socio-political relationships. Thus, we can note that the intimate relationship between David and Jonathan is set forth as a covenant (1 Sam. 18:3; 20:8; 23:18). Elsewhere the D historian presents examples, sometimes contained in earlier sources, of covenant-making activity between two peoples. In 1 Samuel 11:1, the people of Jabesh-gilead request a covenant between themselves and Nahash the Ammonite, although the story goes on to show how his terms were hardly acceptable and how Saul finally delivered the people of Jabesh-gilead from having to make a covenant with Ammon. A second example is in 1 Kings 20:34, where Ahab concludes a covenant or treaty with Ben-hadad, king of Syria. Finally, in 2 Kings 11:4, Jehoiada, the priest of Yahweh, makes a covenant with the Carites, who are possibly the Cherethites, a group loyal to the royal house (2 Sam. 8:18). They are instrumental in seeing that Joash is rightfully crowned as king in the place of the usurper Athaliah.

The main notions of covenant in the D history, however, deal with the covenant with the patriarchs, the covenant with David, and as we have noted, the classic covenant traced to the times of Moses and associated in later reaffirmation ceremonies with the city of Shechem. Beginning with the patriarchs, we can notice in the D history a strong application of his understanding of the covenant in terms of these ancestors. For the historian the term "fathers" (*ăbôt*) commonly refers to the patriarchs Abraham, Isaac, and Jacob, although sometimes it can refer also to the people of the Mosaic era (Deut. 5:2–3). But there can be little doubt that for the D historian the election of Israel began with the patriarchs.

The era of the fathers initiated a relation between God and Israel which was to be decisive for all future events involving the people, for it was here that a special bond was forged between Yahweh and Israel. In some cases, the historian can refer to this close relationship as a covenant with the fathers, as in Deuteronomy 4:31, and 2 Kings 13:23, while elsewhere he passes over an explicit reference to covenant, preferring the verbal phrase "as he swore to our fathers." The latter is the most customary form in the Book of Deuteronomy (Deut. 1:8; 34:4, et passim) where it occurs often in connection with land. It seems apparent that if we are to understand the D historian at this point, he was envisaging an Israel with a special relationship to Yahweh traceable as far back as that history could be remembered. The earliest point of any significance for Israel was the patriarchal era, and the covenant with the fathers bestowed on Israel both a consciousness of the love of God for her and a sense of responsibility and attachment driven deep into her self-consciousness.

Theologically close to this patriarchal covenant was the royal covenant, the "eternal covenant" with David and his dynasty. It would have been far from the mind of the historian to conceive of the establishment of the dynasty of David as having only questionable importance for the covenant between God and Israel. Rather the Davidic era was another great chapter, and indeed an unexcelled one, in the history of the association of God and his people. David did not enter as an interloper into the progression of the covenant through history. His appearance as a critical, historical figure marked a new point in the challenges facing Israel in her election history. Thus it is not surprising that scholars have been able to note how the oracle which provided the basic authentication for the dynasty of David, the so-called "oracle of Nathan the prophet" in 2 Samuel 7:1–29, is impregnated with Deuteronomic additions. The historian saw this covenant with David as decisive and expended no little personal effort to describe it. For him it was of the greatest importance for the history of the kings who followed David, most of whom, however, obstructed the promises contained in that covenant from coming to fruition.

The D historian does not use the term covenant in the oracle of Nathan, but all the realities of a covenant making action are present. The intent of the section is to show how David's house was chosen to be the recipient of the divine promise concerning the future of Israel. Again the D historian did not come at this notion entirely uninfluenced by older traditions, for it seems that Psalm 89, which unquestionably predated his work, had a sizable impact on the composition of 2 Samuel 7. In addition, Psalm 89 mentions specifically the covenant with David as the chosen one of God in Psalm 89:3–4 (cf. 2 Sam. 23:5).

The setting for the oracle of Nathan, however, is the matter of the construction of a proper resting place for the ark of God (2 Sam. 7:2). The D historian's convictions are indicated in the lengthy speech of Nathan in 2 Samuel 7:4–17, as well as in David's reply in 2 Samuel 7:18–29. Here it becomes clear that David will not undertake the building of the Jerusalem temple. This privilege will rather be given to his successor, Solomon. No reasons are given for this disappointing situation, but it is really of little moment since the historian is essentially interested in depicting a David who conformed his life to the will of Yahweh. Although deprived of what would have been an activity passionately sought after by any great ancient Near Eastern monarch, the rejection in no way unsettled David. Rather, what he hears in its place from the prophet Nathan is a promise of the future and strength of his house. Through the confirmation of David as the king, the covenant with all of Israel is made that much firmer (2 Sam. 7:24–27).

However, in neither the covenant with the fathers nor the covenant with David, do we find the most determinative notion of covenant for the D historian. Both of these are important, and certain arguments are built upon them as a foundation (2 Kings 17:21). But the historian's work is informed more by the dynamics of the Mosaic covenant than by these two.

Yet the Mosaic covenant is not simply a repeat of the form found in the earlier traditions of Exodus 20 or 34. Even Deuteronomy 5:1–22, which contains the D historian's version of the covenant at Horeb (Sinai), is presented in a new way reflective of the historian's theological and ethical interests. The section is part of the speech of Moses in the plain of Moab (Deut. 1:1), which is intended to prepare the people of Israel for entry into the land west of the Jordan. With that dramatic setting, the D historian is able to make his most forcible point: the Mosaic covenant was given not only for the sake of the fathers but for "all of us here alive this day" (Deut. 5:3). We can see in the D historian's use of this aspect of the covenant traditions an intention to stress their present efficacy and relevance. It is clear that such an emphasis would lend support to his theological program of serious reform, which he also envisaged as a possibility in the activities supported by Josiah. Consequently, the Book of Deuteronomy contains a good deal of application, based on reflections on the Mosaic covenant.

A further point becomes apparent when we examine the overarching importance of the Mosaic covenant in the D historian's work. It is really under this covenant that he synthesized the elements of the patriarchal and royal covenants discussed previously. In other words, the determinative period for him was that of the revelation to Moses. Thus when he uses the term "fathers," we have already seen that it is not always clear that he means this designation in respect to the patriarchs. Rather the term often appears to reflect back to the entire group of Israel's ancestors, to the period of her formation, all of which are viewed under the perspective of the covenant made with Israel through Moses. If we ask why this Mosaic covenant came to hold such an eminent place in the thinking of the D historian, it is doubtless because of its provisions for internal discipline. Neither the patriarchal nor royal covenants carried through to the responsibilities of Israel. But in the Mosaic covenant that aspect of the relationship was spelled out with detailed clarity.

The influence of the Mosaic covenant can be seen in the third speech of Moses on the other side of the Jordan in Deuteronomy 29:1–29. This lengthy speech is typically Deuteronomic. It begins with the formula "these are the words of the covenant" (Deut. 29:1), the covenant here being seen as a reiteration in Transjordan of the one made with Moses at Horeb. Following a recitation of the great deeds which Yahweh had done for his people (29:2–9), the accent shifts toward the responsibility of Israel (verses 10–29). And that responsibility is epitomized by the call to careful avoidance of the gods of the peoples of the land (verses 16–19). Were Israel not to comply, by assimilating aspects of foreign belief, she would have forsaken the covenant (verse 25) and turned herself over to a desolation as great as that of Sodom and Gomorrah, Admah and Zeboiim (verse 23). This entire chapter ends with a provocative Deuteronomic statement, one which shows how deeply the historian came to view Israel's own obedience to the commandments as an important element attached to the covenant: "The secret things belong to the Lord our God; but the things that are revealed belong to us and to our children for ever, that we may do all the words of this law" (verse 29).

It is this sense of accountability that provides direction for the D historian's use of the concept of covenant throughout his work. We find it in one of the historian's assessments in Judges 2:20, where Israel's many troubles came upon her because they "transgressed my covenant which I commanded their fathers, and have not obeyed my voice." It is present in the Elijah cycle in a section which is undoubtedly from an older source, but which may have been slightly reworked by the D historian. As Elijah meets God at Mount Horeb, he complains that the people of Israel "have forsaken thy covenant" (1 Kings 19:10, 14). And finally, the destruction of the northern kingdom was held by the D historian to have occurred, "because they did not obey the voice of the Lord their God but transgressed his covenant, even all that Moses the servant of the Lord commanded; they neither listened nor obeyed" (2 Kings 18:12).

For the historian, therefore, the primary basis for the relation between Israel and God was to be found in this intimate bond. God was known, as in Solomon's prayer, as the one who keeps his covenant and who shows steadfast love or covenant loyalty (*ḥesed*: 1 Kings 8:23). Israel was to be loyal to some specifically understood demands. It is for this reason that the term covenant, from the side of Israel's accountability, began to move even closer to being equated with the commandments themselves, although we would be misinterpreting the D historian's intent were we to go too far in stressing this point.

This structuring of Israel's history around the framework of an ancient covenant relation, must be seen in connection with the events of the reign of Josiah over Judah. The whole issue has been much discussed, and there now seems to be a consensus among students of Deuteronomy through Kings that the "book of the law" found by

Hilkiah in the Jerusalem temple during the days of Josiah (2 Kings 22:8) must have contained the core of what is our present book of Deuteronomy (Deut. 5—28). It is not without significance that the D history calls this book also the "book of the covenant" (2 Kings 23:2, 21). For whatever its specific relation to the reforms set in motion by Josiah, the recovery of this document, and the theological and ethical inspiration which it produced, left no small impact upon the historian. With this document as his basis, the historian was able to provide an interpretation of the history of Israel by which this history in its various eras, crises, and times of deliverance, could be understood. Also it could set before the listeners of his own time the challenge of what must be done now in order to remain true and obedient to the covenant. Thus he does not take up the idea of covenant and present it objectively or disinterestedly. For him it becomes the most basic organizing principle, the notion on which Israel stands or falls, the premise for any future which might be created for her beyond the chaos of the present.

CHAPTER FIVE

LAW AND GRACE

Behind the different types of covenants which we have examined in the previous chapter lurks a theological problem of cardinal importance. It stems from the D historian's viewpoint regarding the relationship between Israel and God in the covenants which he introduces. At some points we have seen how in his thinking the commandments become an important element in this relationship, while elsewhere a covenant form may simply be based on a spontaneous outpouring of divine goodness. Thus we might wonder about the potential disharmony between a theology of covenant based on grace and a theology in which the requirements laid upon Israel are pulled to the forefront.

Put in another way, what is the relation between law and grace in the D historian's work? Does one or the other of these theological extremes dominate the historian's perspective? Are these contrasting elements primarily in tension with each other, so that the historian, unable to resolve the basic incompatibilities or at least suspensions, maintained the theological polarity? Or did he consciously move them toward some kind of accord? Did the D historian develop a view of the necessity of both commandment and gracious event in the total divine working, and if so how did he understand this necessity? Trying to stay as close to questions which will help to elaborate his own thought, how did he view commandment itself? Did he envisage commandment as an expression of divine graciousness or of threat?

We do well in answering these queries to examine some specific illustrations in the D history and to base our conclusions as approximately as possible on data from the historian's own work. Since this particular problem is one which has greatly occupied theology, it would be easy to misconstrue his viewpoint and to synthesize it under categories which belong to later theological reflection. However, if our consideration of this problem is focused on sections which clearly

represent the D historian's views, we should find our way to discern-
ing the way he handles the tension between grace and law.

We have already seen that one of the forms in which the historian's
ideas comes through is in the speeches which he customarily attributes
to certain key figures and places at critical transition points in the
history of Israel. Thus they are of structural importance in his history. It is in the speeches that the D historian extends himself and
puts into formal expression his theology of Israel and her relation to
God. We shall explore the speeches, then, for what they are able to
show us of the D historian's awareness of the relation between law
and grace. In addition, we shall also look at summary and interpretive sections in his history, where he assesses frequently Israel's relation to God in light of his theological viewpoint. Finally, we shall
examine a number of places where curses, which appear to be expressed in Deuteronomic style and form, also have a bearing upon
our subject.

In Joshua 1:1–9 is a speech of basic importance. It is positioned
by the historian at a turning point, following the death of Moses. It
is now incumbent upon Joshua to take over the responsibilities of
leading Israel through to the completion of a promise which God had
planned for her. This momentous time and task are provided a special dimension by the direct words from God to Joshua.

The speech as a unit is broken at a critical point. Joshua 1:2–6
contains the directive to Joshua to lead the people across the Jordan,
and this section ends in the formula "be strong and of good courage."
The second part begins with verse 7, repeating the formula and then
introducing the summons to meditate upon and to do everything in
the book of the law. This section again is completed with the assurance formula "be strong and of good courage." There is a question
whether these two parts of the unit were both from the D historian,
or whether we have several hands at work here. It is possible that
some expansion of the commandment section in Joshua 1:8 has
occurred. However, this would only suggest that the D historian's
assertions in verse 7 may have been elaborated with greater speci-
ficity by someone supplying a gloss in verse 8. Apart from that single
verse, the unit as a whole seems to reflect the fundamental thought of
the historian.

As we now have it, this section begins with a reflection on the pro-

tective and gracious deeds of God, and then proceeds to introduce
the motif of doing according to all that the law has commanded. In
the first of these two segments the stress is on Yahweh's giving and
action. The land itself is something that he is bestowing upon them
as a gift (Josh. 1:3). Here again the D historian shows how the roots
of his thinking are often deep in the ancient traditions, because the
theme of land is based very early on the notion of promise. In Joshua
1:3 the emphasis on what God spoke (RSV "promised") to Moses
accents the beneficent deeds of God. And finally, even Joshua himself is confronted with the pledge of the fundamental gracious and
sustaining activity of God when his mission is undergirded with the
formula "I will be with you" (verse 5). This formulalike expression
is no peripheral element in the Deuteronomically-conceived speech.
It has its roots in the prophetic salvation oracles, such as in Isaiah
43:1–5. Elsewhere it is found in the prophetic call accounts such as
in Jeremiah 1:8, 19. In every case it is expressive of the gracious,
delivering power of God in which every leader and every individual
Israelite was called to trust.

The second part of the unit is introduced with the particle "only"
in verse 7. We find that word again in 1:18, as in 1:7, connected
with the assertion "be strong and of good courage." It is with that
brief declaration that the particle no doubt originally had its function. But in verse 7 it must be seen as introducing a larger restrictive
clause, "being careful to do according to all the law which Moses my
servant commanded you." In other words, with this particle the D
historian can introduce the segment dealing with Joshua's and Israel's
obedience to the law and commandments. The word "only" is a swing
word allowing the historian to move his thought in a further direction, to introduce a new motif and a new body of material into the
speech. We have here a good illustration of the problem regarding
the relation between the declaration of the gracious deeds of God
and the actions which are compulsory for Israel in maintaining the
covenant.

If the speech is viewed as a whole, it is hardly possible to hold
anything other than that the first segment is the truly constitutive
part. What establishes Joshua's mission and the confidence of a
future for Israel is the word and promise, and these have already

proven their effectiveness in the career of Moses (Josh. 1:3) and the fathers who were before him (1:6). In the first section the relationship does not revolve around a responsibility conceived of in relation to Israel. Yahweh is the actor and everything which lies ahead of Israel is blessed by the consistency of his action. How then is the second segment to be understood in relation to the first?

It would seem that we have two possibilities open to us. One is that the call to do the law and the commandments serves to fill out the life of Israel in the covenant, that it functions as parenesis, as an exhortatory device calling to a life commensurate with the covenant relationship. The other possibility is that it serves also to curb, that it functions as an implicit admonition and even as a threat to Joshua and Israel. In this view the covenant cannot continue to be sustained if Israel fails to fulfill her own duties within its defined limits. Elsewhere it is possible that we may find the law and commandments serving in this second way, but in this speech it is much more the first which appears to be present. The Israel which is being settled by Yahweh in its land must be alert persistently to the definition of its special life in the law which was commanded. This is especially urgent because of the pitfalls which will face her west of the Jordan. The particle "only" introduces that summons, and it is notable that the motivation is not even presented explicitly in terms of threat but rather that "you shall make your way prosperous" and "you shall have good success" (1:8).

At the other end of Joshua's career, at Joshua 23:2–16, is another Deuteronomic speech. The aged leader is portrayed here as having brought the people into Cisjordan and having put their enemies under subjection. The interplay between the theme of gracious deliverance and the admonition to Israel to fulfill her role in the relation with Yahweh is once again important to follow in this speech.

This section is characterized throughout by the style and vocabulary which disinguish the historian. But within the unit we can note several subsidiary segments with their own foci. Thus in Joshua 23:2–5 the stress is once more upon the delivering deeds of God as the one who dispossessed the nations for Israel and fought on her behalf to bring her to the land concerning which he had spoken (RSV "promised") to her. Beginning with verse 6 a new section is introduced with the connective translated as "therefore" in RSV, but which may also simply be rendered as "now." What follows is the command in verses 6–8 to avoid mixing with the peoples and their gods and to remain in allegiance to Yahweh only. With verses 9–10 the delivering power of Yahweh is brought into view once more, and if some scholars who have proposed that the word "love" in verse 11 really means "covenant faithfulness" are correct, then this latter verse reiterates the expectations upon Israel's part.[5] A new element in verses 12–13, however, is that of warning expressed in the form of a lengthy "if" clause. This element is rounded out in the final summation remarks in verses 14–16, in which Yahweh's deeds are noted again. These verses contain, in addition, the warning that were Israel to transgress the covenant, Yahweh could also act in opposite fashion to take everything away that he had given, and even to drive her from the land. This last motif is clearly indicative of conditions during the D historian's own time.

The final speech of Joshua thus contains no unusual elements in its first part. We can note that, like Joshua 1:2–9, it presents the delivering deeds of God as fundamental to the basic relation between God and Israel. The call to serve him by doing all that is in the book of the law (23:6) is hortatory and expresses the significance of Israel's response to the relationship. But in the latter part of this speech, from verses 12–16, we do indeed meet a novel element, that of warning and of threat. It is of basic importance to ask how these "if" sections function in the D historian's theology of relationship.

One of the elements of covenant that recent studies have isolated is that of the blessing and curse formulas which were introduced for specific purposes in ancient covenant making. It is quite possible that the final speech of Joshua in chapter 23 is to be understood in the light of formal covenant-making language; more specifically this speech may have been modeled on the apparently older, formal covenant-making materials in chapter 24. In this case we would have to understand the "if" clauses in the final part of the Joshua speech as formal elements related to the way curses functioned in treaties.

A hasty interpretation of the "if" sections could lead us to interpret the covenant of the D historian as one fundamentally based in obedience to the law, that it is a conditional covenant grounded on Israel's willingness or unwillingness to respond. Were this interpretation pursued, it would be difficult to keep from viewing the responsibility placed upon Israel as foundational for the establishment and continuation of the covenant. We might also see the obedience element as ultimately overpowering the deliverance motif on which the covenant appears to be based.

However, if assertions in the latter part of the speech do indeed derive from formal covenant elements, then their function must be determined in light of that type of usage. That usage seems to be as threat in regard to the *termination* of the covenant, not its *establishment*. The analogy to curses in treaty formulations would undergird this. The constitutive basis of the covenant is not Israel's obedience but the promising action of God which is always the a priori action for anything which is happening to Israel. In the D historian's thought it was God who acted to choose and bring Israel along through her history. Nevertheless, Israel could decide against him and repudiate his actions. Israel could choose death for herself. The "if" clauses are employed by the historian to make that fact lucid and unmistakable. Theologically, therefore, we would have to conclude that Israel does not begin the covenant. God does. However, Israel could fracture it and bring it near to destruction. Perhaps she could even provoke its termination. That possibility is one which the D historian had to consider (see Chapter Nine).

There is in the D history one more lengthy example of direct discourse which gives us insight into his theology of covenant. It occurs in the context of the dedication of the Jerusalem temple (1 Kings 8). The section has been widely recognized as containing Deuteronomic elements. In actuality it consists of three parts: a first-person address of Solomon to the people of Israel in verses 14–21; the prayer of Solomon at the dedication of the temple in verses 22–53; and an expansion of the prayer, perhaps by another person associated with the Deuteronomic movement in verses 54–61.

The first part may be passed over readily. It expresses Solomon's assertion that he has provided a place for the ark of the Lord in constructing the temple at Jerusalem. It is in the prayer of Solomon in verses 22–53 that we can note again some key elements in the D historian's theology of law and grace. The prayer falls into fundamental

parts, the first in verses 22–30 and the second in verses 31–53. In the first segment the emphasis is upon the faithfulness of Yahweh in having kept his promises to David by establishing Solomon as his successor. The motif here is that of the royal covenant and stresses the eternal dynasty of David. With that as a basis, and since Solomon has now constructed the temple, the prayer proceeds to petition that the temple itself might be a special locus for both the presence of God and the place where his forgiveness and providential protection might be sought repeatedly.

The second section in 8:31–53 introduces the notion of the accountability expected of Israel, as well as the punitive activity of God. The section consists of seven hypothetical instances—all rooted in real experience—in which either Israelites or a "foreigner" (8:41–43) might come to make petition at the temple. The cases cited are either a particular sin which might be committed and thus might open the way for disaster, or foreign invasion and captivity. The "sins" which might be committed are in reality failures to do the commandments and statutes. Thus the D historian does not question that the covenant puts a radically serious responsibility and discipline upon Israel, particularly in the times in which he is writing. However, at the same time we can note one of the strong elements which belongs in his theological structure: the petition for forgiveness and the assumption that Yahweh's nature is such that he will forego repeatedly the deserved punishment. When Israel sins he will forgive.

The formula-like expression "hear thou in heaven and forgive the sin of thy people Israel" (8:34, 36, 39, 50) is repeated four times in this prayer reflecting the D historian's theology of the temple. It provides an insight into the historian's concept of the covenant relation which is so central to the basic prayer. This emphasis is undergirded by the only other clear reference to forgiveness in this kind of setting, by a prophet contemporary with the historian (Jer. 31:34; 36:3). For Jeremiah the notion of forgiveness is clearly associated with the covenant in the prophet's words concerning a "new covenant."

Such an emphasis could be present in the D historian's thinking only because his idea of the covenant is grounded on the basic notion that God is the primary actor and maintainer of Israel's covenant bond. To be sure, the responsibilities of Israel are spelled out in the commandments and ordinances, but Israel's role and God's role are qualitatively different. The covenant is not one of simple parity. It originates in generous saving acts and gifts. Thus it is possible for the D historian to extend the idea to its most apparent conclusion: even when Israel might fail, she could "turn" and seek forgiveness which would restore her. The idea is of course not limited to the historian, for we find similar assertions in the calls to repentance and in the salvation oracles of the prophets. However, it takes on a particular importance in the D historian's work, especially with his specific stress on forgiveness.

A discussion of the problem of grace and law must include necessarily two examples which belong not to speeches but to Deuteronomic summations, one in Judges 2:11–23 and the other in 2 Kings 17:7–41. In these sections, too, the D historian's understanding becomes transparent. The section in Judges 2:11–23 would seem to underscore a fundamental idea, that Yahweh remained faithful consistently to the covenant he had made with his people. On their side the people tended toward a pattern of transgression. What is noteworthy in this section, however, is that even the "sore straits" (Judg. 2:15) into which God gave them were not done with the intention of ultimate abandonment. Rather, after a period of chastisement "judges" were raised up to save them from the power of the plunderers. Here again is the stress on the a priori work of God who had acted to establish the bond. In fact, so heavily is the covenant viewed in this way, as a theocentrically based one, that in Judges 2:20 and various places, Yahweh can even refer to it as "my covenant which I commanded their fathers."

The case is similar in 2 Kings 17:7–41 but here the description is entirely of Israel's repeated abandonment of the commandments and her forsaking of the Lord. The section stands out when compared with the earlier record in Judges 2:11–23. By the time of the late monarchy the history of Israel's transgression had precipitated a disaster for which any thoughts about how Yahweh could save them had become smothered. Nonetheless, the basic theology of the D historian is still operative here. Israel could and often did infringe on the covenant contract, in this case to the point of serious calamity.

It is important not to exaggerate the historian's view of law and grace as something wholly unique. Although his style and way of structuring his history are distinctive, yet he himself stood squarely in the traditions of Israel as he had received them. We have seen that the prototypes for the kind of covenant relationship so heavily assumed in the historian's work are to be found both in older Israelite literature, such as Joshua 24, and in ancient Near Eastern treaties. In another direction, the use of the covenant idea in the D history resembles its use in the prophets, and he must at least be understood as having been familiar with the teaching of the prophetic movement.

More important is the theological question of the relation between law and grace. What indeed is the role that the commandments play in the historian's idea of the covenant? First, they are not found as an initial element in the covenant. Rather, what comes first are the benevolent acts of which the D historian gives frequent account. The commandments define the discipline to which Israel is obligated under the relationship, and in that sense phrases such as "transgressing the covenant" (Judges 2:20), or its opposite "keeping the covenant" (1 Kings 11:11) are clearly addressed to Israel. But these expressions ought not be interpreted to mean that the D historian had come to view Israel's obedience or transgression as the essential center of the covenant. These are always the derived elements in the notion of covenant.

The covenant is fundamentally posited on the basis of Yahweh's beneficent acts, and the commandments function as parenesis or negative parameters providing the borders for a life of discipline and commitment.[6] Thus the primary action of God is that of choosing and saving his people, while his negative action of punishment and death, inflicted either by threat or in actuality, belongs to the side of his fundamental work. Therefore it does not really seem correct to place the actions of deliverance on the one hand, and law, punishment, and death on the other, into the same field of God's action.[7] Even Near Eastern treaties seem to have employed stipulations and threats as secondary and derivative, as we have seen and as the following statement suggests: "The ancient treaty was basically an elaborate promise, and the function of the curses attached to the treaty was to make sure that the promise would be kept by invoking the punishment of the gods on the defaulter."[8]

If this ordering is kept in mind, then two things which seem dia-
metrically opposed to each other in the D historian's work might be
understood better. On the one side, the commandments are held by
him to be keepable. In fact, there are times, such as during the age
of Joshua (Judges 2:7), when Israel was viewed as having been
obedient. From this fact we would have to deduce that the listing of
expectations in the form of commandments, ordinances, and statutes
did not inevitably and even fundamentally serve as a threat to Israel.
Often the historian could see Israel responding gladly to them and
forming her communal expression in such a way that she became a
testimony to the nations about her.

On another level, quite distinct from the positive use of the commandments, the D historian could employ freely the ancient curse
form. Here the commandments are shaped not only according to
their positive assertions, but a series of threats appears beside them.
These curses or threats serve in their own way the aim of promoting
a discipline by which Israel's uniqueness could be maintained. At the
same time they functioned as an attempt to motivate Israel. If it is
here that they may have broken down ultimately (cf. Rom. 5:20),
it should not prevent us from looking seriously at the D historian's
attempt to address Israel with a call to renewed life in the covenant.
In any case it was not the only manner by which he attempted to
induce Israel to entrust herself wholeheartedly to her relation with
Yahweh. Elsewhere Israel is called simply to love him and his
commands (Deut. 6:4–9).

Only if we see the importance for the historian of the promissory
nature of Yahweh's covenant, can we understand how he managed
some harmony in the use of both the royal Davidic and the Sinai
covenants. Like the prophets, the historian could distinguish the
benevolent saving deeds as the primary activity of God. In his thinking even the divine disappointment and wrath over Israel's persistent
failures are mitigated repeatedly by saving events which vouchsafe
that prior promise. For him grace is the initial act which constituted
Israel. The laws provide structure for what the community is to be.
The historian saw the necessity of an internal discipline, and thus the
Mosaic stipulations were essential. God could also punish and even
reject. But as far as his understanding of the punitive activity of God

was concerned, the D historian seems to have come within sight of comprehending what the theologians of the Reformation era later were to designate God's "proper" (grace) and his "foreign" work (law, death). The law could bring death, but only as the foreign work of God. At the same time, for the historian the laws and commandments could be kept also as a response to the gracious deeds of a delivering God by a willing people. In this understanding he differed from what was to become the position of the later theologians of law and gospel.

CHAPTER SIX

PROPHECY AND FULFILLMENT

Undoubtedly an outstanding feature of the D historian's work is the fundamental historical viewpoint itself which can be seen throughout the work and which gives it striking integrity and unity. The composer of this great work had profound historiographic interests. He set out to obtain a fuller understanding of Israel's history from the time she settled in the land until the days of the destruction of both the northern and southern states. He desired to comprehend larger patterns and movements in that history and to attempt some causal explanations of what ultimately had brought Israel to the point of calamity. In the pursuit of such objectives he showed himself an astute observer and thinker—considering the fact that such historiographic interests were not greatly developed at the time he was living.

It must be admitted that his historical views in the final analysis were highly theological and that he could not be considered a precursor of modern historical thinking. He does not trace events for their implicit, historical value. He does not carry out his plan of writing a comprehensive interpretation of ancient Israel by means of objectively studied sources and data concerning political and social events, although he incorporates into his work a document such as the Succession Document (2 Sam. 9—20; 1 Kings 1—2) which displays some of these features. For the D historian the history of Israel makes sense only if seen as the history of a special people with a responsibility, a people dependent on what God has spoken and promised. Her history is a history under the word, and so the juxtapositions for which he looks are not those of a secular historian, but rather the manner in which a word spoken previously has opened up to bring about events which fulfilled it at a subsequent time.

As can be seen in various older materials which he employed, the

D historian was familiar with a concept of the word which had long before his time lodged itself in the consciousness of Israel. In this ancient view the word possessed the potentiality to effect what it expressed verbally. This prevalent ancient Near Eastern concept of the power of the word is difficult but important to understand since it follows a quite different path from modern notions about the meaning of word. It is perhaps not an oversimplification to say that modern people function with a much greater distance between words and reality than the ancients did. For the latter the power of an utterance to lead to a concrete result reduced the dichotomy between word and thing. This view can be seen most readily in the common Hebrew term for word, *dābār*, which can be used to denote either word or event.

The D history simply applied this idea of the powerful word to many specific instances. Judges 11 provides a case in which the word shaped in the form of a vow has a special kind of force. The old story of Jephthah and the tragic implications of his vow is full of irony. Nonetheless, the story in its continuous transmission to the times of the D historian was aimed not only at explaining what might have been an annual ritual featuring a lament over Jephthah's daughter (Judg. 11:39-40); it was equally intent on projecting the strength of a vow as an inherently powerful word. At least it took for granted, according to the old Israelite view, that even if Jephthah had promised rather compulsively to offer as a burnt offering the first person to meet him after his victory over the Ammonites, nonetheless that vow was inexorable in its effect (Judg. 11:31, 35). The word once spoken and legitimated by placing it in the sphere of God's hearing, was ineradicable. Thus the story draws to its conclusion with an ending grounded not so much in a sense of fatedness known from similar Greek stories, but rather in a notion about the relation of man's word to the word of God, one in which word is not understood casually but as implicitly effective.

In these older traditions, not only is the word of a human being full of this potential power to create some particular condition or outcome in the future, but the same extends to the realm of divine communications. In fact, it is here that we can find some old materials, used by the D historian, employing a similar mode of thinking. One incident of this type used by the historian is the archaic tradition of the Samson story (Judg. 13). In this account the wife of Manoah is met by "a man of God" who offers to her the news that she is to give birth to a son (verse 3). In this old tradition an event such as the birth of an important figure like Samson could be announced by a word. It was the function of the word to precede the event, and actually the thing could not happen unless the word was present previously to create it. This is substantiated later when the same heavenly announcer is addressed by Manoah with the statement: "Now when your words come true . . ." (verse 12). Such an orientation would have been favorable to the D historian's way of thinking, for it was just this kind of interplay between word and event which supplied the basis for his historical presentation.

The Bochim incident, at which we have looked several times, shows a similar way of thinking (Judg. 2:1–5). The heavenly messenger speaking on behalf of Yahweh provides a word of evil news to his hearers in the face of their refusal to obey. This word is so inherently powerful and capable of coming to fulfillment that the people react with weeping (verse 4). But an account which brings us close to the historian's own view is that of the prophet Micaiah's encounters in 1 Kings 22. This story is an interesting prophetic tradition dealing with the authenticity of a prophet and the grounds of his truthfulness. The tense episode between the prophet who delivers the genuine word and the suspicious and frantic king is understandable only if the inherent power of the prophet's words to create the situation which they communicate is viewed as a genuinely disturbing factor.

Thus it was in the potency of such things as oaths and vows, or curses, that a basic concept of the word was rooted. This notion carried over into a larger understanding in which the events affecting the history of Israel occurred as the outcome of a previously uttered word. The schema of promise and fulfillment, found at many places in the historian's work, is based upon a concept of the intrinsically powerful word. The same can be said for its opposite, the intimations of disaster and their outcomes. No doubt the D historian was in some measure indebted to the prophetic tradition of "the word of Yahweh" in this kind of emphasis, for it was in the circle of the prophets that this far-reaching understanding of word and event was developed in its depth. The relation of the D historian to the prophetic movement is an intriguing problem, and one which is not entirely clear in its lines. But the close affinity that the Deuteronomic style has with certain portions of the Book of Jeremiah, and the probable relation that both the prophets and historian had to the reform of Josiah suggest apparent contacts. All of this simply backs up the observation that the historian's view of the word shared in some sense that of the prophets.

That view of the word is sketched out in the important section in Deuteronomy 18:15–22. Here in the core material of the Book of Deuteronomy the ideal prophet is seen to be no less a one than Moses. What is granted to the prophetic spokesman, then, is the genuine word of Yahweh. His word will be distinguishable in its truth from the unauthorized words uttered by false prophets; the criterion is whether the word actually fulfills itself in event or not. For those who presume to speak in the name of Yahweh, but without truly having a word from him, what is spoken will not come to pass, and thus it will also not be true (18:21–22). While this is put negatively, its obverse is implied, that the genuinely prophetic word is one which authenticates itself through what comes to pass in the wake of the uttered word (cf. Amos 3:6–8).

As we examine the D history itself with references to this concept, it soon becomes evident that the previously uttered word and its fulfillment function in a significant structural way in his historical outlook. Although the basic notion is not that of the D historian's, nonetheless he puts it to a particular usage in his comprehensive work. In various blocks of material which are identifiable as his own contribution, the historian exhibits the basic schema of promise or prediction and definitive outcome. Often this interpretation is provided for epochal events which, to his mind, represented turning points in Israel's course through history. But what is especially worthy of note is how much this interpretation, which owes so much to the prophetic tradition and to an older Israelite understanding of the power of the word, is employed by the historian in his unique way to organize a history which could be both useful and instructive.

The first section in which we can see this schema operating is in the final speech of Joshua (Josh. 23:1–16), which has been noted already as a contribution of the historian himself. Particularly in verses 14–16 appears the historian's view of Israel's history as a destiny forged by the promises of Yahweh. Joshua says, "You know in your hearts and souls, all of you, that not one thing has failed of all the good things which the Lord your God promised concerning you; all have come to pass for you, not one of them has failed" (v. 14). Important here is the assertion that the events which happen to Israel grow out of the word of Yahweh (cf. Josh. 1:3). Israel's history does not unfold according to some sort of predetermined law of history, nor are the events affecting her arbitrary ones. Her past, present and future are comprehended in the word of Yahweh. That word both creates her story and illuminates it as it occurs.

The D historian had a clear sense of temporality. Israel lived in time and history, and yet across the large stretches of time her vocation and destiny remained constant. As we see him reflecting on this, the historian's accent falls often on the graciousness of Yahweh who was with her unfailingly. Yahweh is one who gave her successive promises about her future. His dependability is stressed throughout, because he was faithful to those promises and brought them about in due time. It was the privileged calling of certain persons to convey these promises to Israel, and among the group of such spokesmen were Moses (Josh. 1: 13–15), Joshua (Josh. 23: 14–16), some of the judges (Judg. 6:8–10) and especially the prophets. The foremost vocation of all of these was to witness to the trustworthiness of the divine promise. The understanding of the divine word of promise and fulfillment had its basis in this consciousness of a faithful God. That understanding of God had to be modified by a further awareness that this God could utter curse as well as promise. However, this in no sense obliterated the fact that the fundamental comprehension of God lay in the knowledge of him as the faithful one. How could it be otherwise for a historian who knew the ancient traditions about the faithful assurances of Yahweh to the ancestors of Israel?

We can see this understanding of Yahweh's reliable promises in two places especially, both of them credited to the D historian. The first is in 2 Samuel 7 in the oracle given to David. This oracle has been recognized as containing a capsulized form of the historian's basic understandings of Israel's history. The speech of Nathan is permeated with references to God's faithful words which have been or are to be realized in action. Yahweh has been with David wherever he has gone; he will now make his name as one of the great ones of the earth (2 Sam. 7:9). He has also been with Israel and now promises to bring to fulfillment the pledge made to them, to establish them upon a place where they will no longer bear the harrassment of their enemies. The steadfastness of the promise is underscored in that Yahweh will build the house of David whose successor will be his own son and whose throne will be founded into perpetuity.

The second passage which concentrates on the faithful promises is the prayer of Solomon in 1 Kings 8:22–40, a clearly Deuteronomic component. Yahweh is a God who has faithfully watched over the things which were declared to David; with his hand he has "fulfilled it this day" (v. 24). That this prayer is associated with the dedication of the temple in Jerusalem shows how deeply the conviction of Yahweh's faithful promises was tied to the solidarity of the Jerusalem sanctuary. Here at this place, which was central to the historian's conception of the presence of Yahweh, there was preserved this theology of the divine promise. There was an old tradition about the inviolability of Zion, to which prophets such as Isaiah subscribed (Isa. 2:2–4; 10:5–19; 17:12–14; 29:1–8). The historian took up this old tradition of the temple and connected it with the enduring word of Yahweh. The temple itself was the fulfillment of a promise, but also here the word of God's continuing promise to Israel was guarded faithfully.

The history of Israel was thus conceived as being spread out along an expanded string of promises and their culminations. Although highly theological in character, this viewpoint allowed the historian to achieve a coherent understanding of the significance of events. A further factor entered the scheme to differentiate the D historian's understanding from all others who viewed similarly the history of Israel. For him the action of God was performed not only in saving deeds. Yahweh was also one who could hurl unexpected and terrible acts into the face of his people's experiences. For this historian it appeared to be an oversimplification, a naive glorification of the history of Israel, to conceive of it in terms of the inevitable protection and preservation of Yahweh; the judgment and curse of Yahweh were also powers with which to be reckoned (see Chapter Five).

It appears that this judgment side of Yahweh's activity always had to be voiced by the historian, especially when he found reason to speak of the long-term promises of God to Israel. Thus he guarded the promise from becoming a pledge with no call for responsibility and commitment. In the section mentioned previously, Joshua 23:14–16, the reference to Yahweh's faithfulness in fulfilling everything promised to Israel is followed by the exhortation that just as all the good things vouchsafed by Yahweh have become reality, so Israel should know that if she "transgresses the covenant," the anger of Yahweh will arise against her, and what has been fulfilled for her sake will vanish from her.

As the historian formed his presentation of the sacred history from older traditions, this dimension could be highlighted again and again. Either Israel's collective disobedience or the failures of her rulers would put the negative divine word into effect. Such a thought is present in the word spoken against the house of Eli which came to fulfillment (1 Sam. 3:12–14). Again when the dead Samuel is summoned for advice by Saul through the medium at Endor, Samuel responds in Deuteronomic fashion, "The Lord has done to you as he spoke by me; for the Lord has torn the kingdom out of your hand, and given it to your neighbor, David" (1 Sam. 28:17). The word spoken beforehand brings about the fulfillment, in this case a negative outcome.

Often such statements include the conditions attached to Israel's covenant, so that the promise of something in the future is contingent upon Israel's faithfulness to her part of the relationship. At this point occur "if" clauses which must be interpreted in the entire framework of the historian's thought. But it is evident that such qualifications are present, and that a promised future can indeed be deflected or even wholly changed by an Israel unwilling to conform to her unique vocation. Besides Joshua 23:16, "if" clauses are found in promises of the future of David's throne in 1 Kings 2:4, and the building of the temple by Solomon in 1 Kings 6:12. Such a notion was fundamental to the speech of Moses in Deuteronomy 26:16–19. Thus at the great turning points in the history of Israel's leaders Moses, Joshua, David, and Solomon, we find the reaffirmation of the promise with its accompanying responsibilities.

Such an emphasis tied together the historian's understanding of this scheme with a basic theological interest. With that always in the background, his reflection on promise and fulfillment could lead also to some concrete cases in which events were spoken of before and then fulfilled in the context of later happenings. Examples of this abound, especially in the books of Kings. In 1 Kings 11:31 the prophet Ahijah of Shiloh delivers a word in which the house of Solomon and the kingdom of Judah will find the ten northern tribes torn away from the kingdom. The event comes to its fulfillment when Rehoboam acts foolishly to alienate the people of the north. "So the king did not hearken to the people; for it was a turn of affairs brought about by the Lord that he might fulfil his word, which the Lord spoke by Ahijah the Shilonite to Jeroboam the son of Nebat" (1 Kings 12:15; cf. 14:18; 15:29).

Again the historian's framework of prior word and subsequent action is seen in 1 Kings 13:1–4, where the rise of Josiah and his reforming activity were spoken of long before by "a man of God." The section shows the hand and thinking of the historian and cannot be pressed as an actual historical utterance prior to Josiah's time. Along similar lines Zimri wrought destruction on the house of Baasha "according to the word of the Lord" spoken by a prophet named Jehu (1 Kings 16:12). Hiel of Bethel built Jericho and sacrificed his son as a foundation offering according to the word of the Lord given earlier through Joshua (1 Kings 16:34; Josh. 6:26). Elijah speaks according to Yahweh's word beforehand that the jar of meal and the cruse of oil belonging to the woman at Zarephath would not run out (1 Kings 17:16). The house of Ahab especially faced the irrefutable word, that because of this king's sins the dogs would lick the blood of both Ahab and Jezebel (1 Kings 21:19–24)—a judgment word opening with a prophetic messenger formula (1 Kings 21:19) and seen as fulfilled when the events actually come about (2 Kings 9:36–37; 10:10, 17).

In the Elisha cycle of stories we find this prophet performing an unusual act of purifying the water supply of the city by dropping some salt into a bowl of water. Even this act was done and had its consequent effect "according to the word which Elisha spoke" (2 Kings 2:22). Jeroboam II's (786–746 B.C.) policies of expanding the empire were foretold by the prophet Jonah, son of Amittai (2 Kings 14:25), while in a Deuteronomic passage the Lord's promise to Jehu was that his sons would occupy the throne to the fourth generation, a word which found its fulfillment according to the historian's notation (2 Kings 15:12). Both Hezekiah's personal health, as well as the far-flung tragedies his kingdom was much later to suffer, are the subjects of words from Yahweh (2 Kings 20:9, 16–19). Manasseh's intolerably evil reign, as we saw in Chapter Two, was especially viewed as a cause of the catastrophe of 587 B.C. The account of his reign is assessed with such a word of judgment beforehand (2 Kings 21:10–12), fulfilled in the destruction of Jerusalem (2 Kings 24:2).

How are we to consider this understanding of Israel's and Judah's history in the light of words which announce beforehand what is to occur and then summarize the fulfillment of such a word in the light of later events? First, it is important to recall that in the old traditions of Israel, such as we have preserved in the Jahwist or Elohist sources, the notion of promise was a strong one. A typical example would be the J tradition's portrayal of Yahweh's promises to Abraham in Genesis 12:1–4. Thus, far from setting forth an entirely new notion of the word of Yahweh directing Israel, the D historian used this notion in a special way. Not only does he present the certainties found in Yahweh's words at many points; he shows also how these words are filled out consistently in their basic intent, and how events which were spoken of beforehand have found their true fulfillment. From the D historian we have received that ideal of prophecy and fulfillment which had an impact upon later movements within Judaism and on the New Testament.

But there was a second influence. It came from the prophets who were especially schooled and charismatically endowed to give words to Israel and Judah about their futures. The unique types of judgment or salvation oracles given by the prophets have left their imprint upon the historian's presentation. What is different in his case is his application of such an insight across a large part of Israel's history, so that all of Israel's life does indeed become a history under the word delivered by those specially selected to speak Yahweh's words and to put into effect his plans. We have noted a few cases where the formal types of prophetic utterance are present in the D historian's work (1 Kings 21:17–19).

But what is particularly significant in the D historian's work is that the word of Yahweh, always involved in the events affecting Israel, is a word both of salvation and judgment. There is no single word for "promise" or "promises" in the historian's work. We find only formulas such as "according to the word which Yahweh spoke through. . . ." But Yahweh's word can either be a promissory one in a strictly positive sense, or one which implies threat and even certifies the nearness and inevitability of judgment. Both uses are widespread throughout the work as our examples have shown. Nonetheless, the fundamental word of promise to Israel in her election and in the covenant was the basic platform for her calling and self-understanding. The second word, that of promised threat and effectual judgment, though a serious word, is not constitutive of her life. It is found whenever Yahweh turned against Israel because of her violation of the covenant commands. Such words of judgment lie among the pages of the D history as exhortatory, seemingly to clear the slate and lay open a new time in which faithfulness will be found again.

For the D historian, the word of Yahweh is a live, effective, and engaging word which is spoken through his chosen ones. So important is this word that the events of Israel's history can be understood only when they are seen as a confirmation of the divine word and its effects.

CHAPTER SEVEN

LAND

In his use of the land theme the D historian fell heir to a concept with a rich history in ancient Israel. Yet he gave this notion new dimensions in the creative fashion which characterizes so many aspects of his work. The idea of the land serves an axial function through his work, especially since the historian labored under the conditions of the exile of Israel from that land and the loss of the land to foreign invaders. It is not surprising that in some respects the D history is a look backward to understand the nature of the land promise and Israel's long occupation of it prior to the events which scattered her from that solid place.

In the earlier traditions the land was one element among several of the promises of Yahweh. The Jahwist's tradition of promises to Abraham incorporated the land theme along with those of numerous offspring and an assurance of the eventual blessing of Israel by her neighbors (Gen. 12:1–3, 7). The successors of the patriarch were seen to carry on these promises, Isaac in Genesis 22:17 (E) and Jacob in Genesis 28:13 (J/E). Eventually when the Hebrews left Egypt, their escape was to find its strongest explanation as a movement out in the direction of the promised land (Exod. 3:17, J). Among the priestly circles of Israel the notion of the land as Yahweh's own possession given to Israel out of promise and trust, led to strict ordinances protecting the use of the land in its allotment and ownership (Num. 34:2; Lev. 25:23, P).

Thus the D historian had access to a notion with a rich history. One thing which becomes clear in his work is that he elevated this theme to the center of his consideration. He does not show a comparable interest in the other elements of Genesis 12:1–3. It is in the theme of the gift of the land that the historian's estimate of Israel's special relation to Yahweh rests. Here was Yahweh's most intimate promise to her from ancient times onward. It was here that her sense of peoplehood, of covenant, and the significance of her history could indeed be realized.

There are several lines which must be pursued in looking more closely at the D historian's use of the land theme. First, in his view the land was a gift to Israel from God. This is evident in the straightforward address attributed to Moses in Deuteronomy 6:11 but representing the historian's own conceptions. In this section Moses is said to remind Israel that when she enters the land, she will begin to possess cities which she did not build, occupy houses well stocked with materials which Israel herself did not place there, and tend vineyards, use cisterns, plant fields—none of which were originally her own. The land she is about to possess is "the good land which the Lord swore to give to your fathers."

Such an understanding of the land as a gift could lead to various misunderstandings. Taken at face value the conviction that Yahweh gave the land to Israel as a possession would raise questions concerning the justice of this act. Since the land was occupied previously, and since in order to possess it Israel had to displace peoples such as the Canaanites who were there previously, the problem of the legitimacy of such action would arise. From a modern perspective the entire activity might be viewed as another migratory movement of a people in search of elbow-room or living space, legitimated by an appeal to special election. In response to this view, one might point to the frequent assertions about the direct hand of God in this activity. However, some might discount this response by pointing to parallels to the claims of land among many different cultural groups. The difficulty of this question is not easy to resolve.

It is important to inquire whether the D historian himself grappled at all with the problem of taking the land from its prior occupants and its being presented outright to his own people. Does he give evidence of having thought about the problems of the justice of this claim? Are there indications of a wider perspective in which he understood the appropriation of tracts of land both east and west of the Jordan?

There is some evidence, in the first place, that the historian did view the problem from a vantage point which was at least aware of this matter. His perspective is implied in the lengthy speech attributed to Moses in the early chapters of Deuteronomy. Here it is asserted several times that Yahweh was not only one who oversaw and legitimated the appropriation of land to the people of Israel. He also did the same for the sons of Lot to whom he gave the land of Moab as a possession (Deut. 2:9). He did similarly for the sons of Esau, the Edomites (Deut. 2:5, 22), and the Ammonites. Even those called the Caphtorim in Deuteronomy 2:23, apparently a group linked to the Philistines, were engaged in the activity of dispossession. Their ventures coincided with the plans of Yahweh as surely as did his similar works among the Israelites. Particularly noteworthy is the statement about the sons of Esau who displaced the Horites who were previously in the region. The notation reads: "The Horites also lived in Seir formerly, but the sons of Esau dispossessed them, and destroyed them from before them, and settled in their stead" (Deut. 2:12). This observation evidently betrays some thought on the part of the historian devoted to the problem of land taking. It was not unimportant to him that analogies for Israel's possession of the territory of the Canaanites could be found among some of her closest neighbors, most of whom also occupied lands formerly inhabited by other peoples.

Thus there does seem to be here a conscience which reflects on the problem of the possession of the land, even if the historian does not carry this reflection very far. His thoughts may not satisfy many modern people, but if read in the light of conditions during the Iron Age in Palestine, when displacement was an everyday event, they do suggest a responsiveness to the human and moral dimensions of such activity. There seems to be little other explanation for his references to parallel situations of land occupation than that he was struggling with the implications of his people's occupation of the territories of another people. That he could even interpret the possession of lands by the neighboring peoples as having been carried out under the guidance of Yahweh highlights his engagement with that problem even further.

Another aspect of the historian's thought counteracted what could have degenerated into crude notions of displacement. Throughout his work the references to the land are enveloped in a spirit of humble thankfulness. The historian calls into question repeatedly any notion that the land was something that could be taken for granted. Rather Israel had received it by means of a beneficent act of Yahweh. For the historian Israel needed to be reminded constantly that she did not come to the land by her own power. She was really an insignificant people, hardly capable of being called a people at all (Deut. 7:7). It was not by her might and strategy that she entered the land; she was led by Yahweh to her possession.

Once the gift was recognized as such, the historian could hold the view that Israel should spare nothing in the way of courageous action to take what had been given to her. In his view this forcefulness of the taking of the land, along with the heavy emphasis on its gift nature, provides something of an internal contradiction. On the one hand, the land is not something which Israel possesses in her own right. Yet, on the other hand, she is encouraged to undertake its occupation with determination. Her vacillation in taking it would give evidence for a lack of trust in and obedience to Yahweh (Josh. 1:2–11). The tension between these two notions remains throughout the historian's work.

The relation of the incoming people of Israel to the previous occupants of the land is brought out most strongly in the double-sided meaning of a word which can be translated either as "possess" or "dispossess" (*yaraš*), depending on the context. In its first sense it is usually employed for possessing the land which Yahweh is giving as a fulfillment of the pledge to the fathers (Josh. 1:11; 24:8; Judg. 2:6). Obversely it denotes the dispossession of the peoples who dwelt formerly in the land (Judg. 11:23). No doubt through his usage of this Hebrew term, the historian would have been aware that the possession of the land meant also the dispossession of its peoples (Judg. 11:24).

But if Israel were to take her land, an important problem is what the D historian had in mind by the land promised to the fathers. How did he conceive of the geographical extent of this territory? We know that there were older traditions about the land which perceived its boundaries as reaching from the brook of Egypt, probably near the northern Sinai peninsula, as far as the Euphrates River (Gen. 15:18–

19, E). These ideas of the boundary of Israel could not be normative, however, although the historian gave expression to them (Josh. 1:4). They reflected more a crystallized version of territorial expansion stemming from the momentary advances of the kingdom of Israel under David. Thus they did not conform to reality, which more commonly found the Israelites confined to the areas west of the Jordan River. The eighth century B.C., however, witnessed the expansion of control to regions similar to those during the age of David and Solomon (2 Kings 14:24–25).

The areas in the historian's mind were largely those concentrated west of the Jordan River, in the region sometimes called Cisjordan (Josh. 1:2). This was an area inhabited by a heterogeneous population, the names of which are listed by the historian as Canaanites, Amorites, Hittites, Hivites, Perizzites and Jebusites (Deut. 20:17; Josh. 12:8; Judg. 3:5; 1 Kings 9:20). It is noteworthy that his pictures of heterogeneity correspond with the cultural picture derived from archaeology which also indicates that during the Iron Age the population of Palestine was diverse. At the same time, the historian considered several regions in Transjordan as part of the land allotment to Israel. These included, in particular, territories which were apportioned to the tribes of Reuben, Gad, and the half-tribe of Manasseh (Deut. 3:12–17; Josh. 13:8–32; 22:1–4). On the other hand, some of the territories in Transjordan were explicitly excluded from occupation since they had been distributed by Yahweh to such peoples as the Horites, Edomites and Moabites (Deut. 2:8–22).

One of the important sources which was incorporated by the historian into his work and which had a bearing on his presentation of the land theme, was the list of tribal boundaries. As we have noted above, the boundary lists have been joined with a second roster, a list of cities. Both of these are found in Joshua 13—21. It seems that the historian's rhetorical and theologized narratives regarding the land were influenced by some of the older data available to him in such lists. Particularly illuminating is the way he worked these rosters in at just the points where they are found presently in his history. Thus the movement in his historical work begins with Moses' exhortatory speech in Deuteronomy, proceeds from there to the narrative accounts of conquest in Joshua 1—12, and finally is followed by the placement of lists at just this location. The latter serve to show how the occupation of the land was carried out with a sense of order and a spirit of completeness. What was promised in the pledges to the fathers comes to fulfillment in the assignment of specific territories to each of the tribes of Israel. Even the details of boundaries, such as running from the edges of wadis, next to streams, across the ridges of hills, or from villages and cities, give extra emphasis to the consummation of the land theme as the most important of the ancient assurances to Israel.

It is not surprising that one of his most important ideas is repeated often in the historian's editing of the boundary lists. This is the notion of the land as an "inheritance" (*naḥᵃlâ*) provided by Yahweh for Israel, and indeed for specific tribes. We find a concentrated use of this word in two places in particular, the Book of Deuteronomy (Deut. 4:38; 19:14; 29:8) and in the framework the historian provides for the tribal boundary and city lists (Josh. 13—21). Not all examples can be cited here but several can be singled out to illustrate the point. In a speech of Yahweh set at the beginning of the lists, Joshua is commanded to allot the land to Israel "for an inheritance" (Josh. 13:6). Then the term is used further to define specific territories assigned to individual tribes, such as the inheritance of Reuben, Gad, and half-Manasseh (Josh. 13:8). Interestingly the tribe of Levi is noted as receiving no inheritance (Josh. 13:33) since it was dedicated to the service of Yahweh in special ways among all the tribes (Deut. 18:2; Josh. 13:14; 14:4), although this tribe did receive specific cities in which to live (Josh. 21:1–42).

The general introduction to the apportionment of areas west of the Jordan River, at Joshua 14:1–5, uses the plural of the term stating "these are the inheritances which the people of Israel received in the land of Canaan" (Josh. 14:1). It depicts further the allocation of lands by means of lots (Josh. 14:2; 16:1; 17:1; 18:11). Altogether, nine and one-half tribes received territories in this manner in Cisjordan, while two and one-half tribes received similarly their alloted lands in Transjordan. Such a division by means of lots was performed for the tribes consecutively (Josh. 18:11—19:51) and is said to have been carried out by the priest Eleazar, as well as by Joshua, before the door of the sanctuary at Shiloh (Josh. 19:51). The tradition is an old one, but it is noteworthy how aptly the D historian has worked it into his presentation.

With this material having reached its conclusion, the historian found it appropriate to add his own comments, as he did in Joshua 21:43–45. Here he sees the entire partitioning of the land, exemplified in the old lists, against the background of the divine completion of promises made to the fathers. With the settlement of the land in this manner the historian could comment that "not one of all the good promises which the Lord made to the house of Israel had failed; all came to pass" (Josh. 21:45).

In this same section of Deuteronomic summary the historian introduces yet another interpretive notion important for his understanding of the land: the possession of the land as a time and place of "rest" ($m^e n\hat{u}h\hat{a}$). The significance of the term "rest" for the historian can be seen in Deuteronomy 12:9, where it appears parallel with "inheritance." In that same verse an exhortation from Moses in Deuteronomic style states that the people have not yet come to their rest, or to put it another way, they have not yet taken possession of the land and settled it (see Ps. 95:11). At the opposite end of things, but now in the context of the Jerusalem temple, Yahweh is praised for having "given rest to his people Israel, according to all that he had promised" (1 Kings 8:56). These words are part of Solomon's dedicatory prayer, and they illustrate the fundamental viewpoint of the D historian: the gift of land along with the centrality of the temple has brought Israel to a consummation in her calling and destiny. In this sense it may not be amiss to say that the historian interprets the possession of the land and its accompanying "rest" as a form of eschatological realization. Indeed it is just this aspect of the notion that a later writer took up and carried some steps further (Heb. 4:1–13).

All that has been said to this point demonstrates the basic importance of the land theme in the historian's work. There is yet another aspect to his use of this notion which stands out in his work: the land becomes a point of testing for Israel. Here can be seen the convergence of the basic theological concern of the D historian for an Israel obedient to the one God, Yahweh, and the ancient idea of the gift of the land. In uniting these two notions, the historian may be said to have combined a concern for the stipulations of the Sinai covenant with the land theme, which was traditionally conceived of as a benevolent pledge on the part of Yahweh.[9] As we have seen, that feature of the land promise is still present in the historian's work and lies behind the oft-used expression "the land promised to your fathers." At the same time he interjects a summons to obedience, to a committed response to Yahweh's gift, and the joining of this motivation to the idea of the gracious gift of land represents one of the novel contributions of the historian to the historical understanding of Israel.

The basic platform for such an understanding of an Israel exhorted to obedience in the face of the gift of the land appears in Deuteronomy 6:10–25. The gift of the land will be an experience of unquestioned generosity on the part of Yahweh when he finally brings his people to occupy it. But the rehearsal of this fact in the moving passage at Deuteronomy 6:10–11, is transformed when the imperative "take heed" occurs (Deut. 6:12). The remainder of the section spells out the responsibilities of Israel, and challenges her to a loyalty to the commandments. While it may be somewhat misleading to use the word "conditional" for such assertions about the gift of the land along with a call to obedience, there is nonetheless a clear linkage between the two which places a heavy onus upon Israel's response. The divine intention to bring Israel to her land cannot come to fulfillment without an Israel dedicated to the covenant with her God. Her disobedience will frustrate the divine promises just as it will elicit the anger of Yahweh (Deut. 6:15).

The same can be seen in the speech of Joshua in Joshua 23:1–16, in which he recalls for "all Israel" the manner in which Yahweh had driven out the nations before her and alloted to each tribe an inheritance in the land (Josh. 23:4). Such protection Yahweh will continue to give according to his word to Israel (Josh. 23:5). But that very fact lays upon Israel the responsibility to keep all that is written in the book of the law, that is, to uphold the covenant statutes and to align herself in devotion only with Yahweh and not with the foreign gods in the land (Josh. 23:6–8). Were Israel to spurn such a vocation, she would find Yahweh withdrawing his care and turning her over to the persecution of the enemy (Josh. 23:12–13). Above all, she would experience an inversion of the gift of the land and her settlement of it by perishing "from the good land which he has given to you" (Josh. 23:16). A comparable admonition is implicit in the dedicatory prayer of Solomon, expressed here as an accomplished fact, that the people had indeed been taken away from the land as captives (1 Kings 8:46–51).

If the D history does embody an inclusive, retrospective interpretation of Israel as a people and of the events which were most critical for her self-understanding, then the notion of the land is a particularly crucial point at which we can see the historian at work. The land was, in fact, only one item which had perished before the invasion of the Babylonian forces in the early sixth century B.C. Gone also were the temple and the old monarchical order of David, once believed to be irremovable. But it was the loss of the land which brought special tragedy and which the historian seems to be at great pains to understand. How is it that a promise once so powerfully believed in, so formative for Israel's relationship to Yahweh through the long years of settlement, could be swept away in the suddenness of attack and captivity?

The historian's grasp of that problem led him to account for it by recourse to a continuous series of unfaithful and disobedient acts traceable back to the earliest times. The land was never a free grant offered without attendant accountability. It was, to be sure, a testimony, a sign of God's gracious intentions toward Israel. It was a living and compelling symbol of the constancy and reliability of that relationship. Nonetheless, the relationship was not wholly from one side; Israel also had her part to carry out. She too was called to participate in the covenant in a way that would witness to her seriousness and her faithfulness. Through the long years following her entry into Cisjordan, years in which she encountered routinely the testings of the peoples and cults still remaining in the land, she seems to have moved ineluctably toward a rejection of the covenant bond. Her kings, apart from only one or two, provoked her to forsake the statutes and ordinances which defined her special life.

When the lengthy history of her occupation of the land came to an end, when Judah alone was left and approaching her demise, the historian could only comment with words brief and yet reflective of his passionate appraisal: "Surely this came upon Judah at the command of the Lord, to remove them out of his sight, for the sins of Manasseh, according to all that he had done . . . for he filled Jerusalem with innocent blood, and the Lord would not pardon" (2 Kings 24:3-4). The loss of her territories represented also the disappearance of a cherished basis for her collective life—the land as a sign of the presence and protection of her God.

CHAPTER EIGHT

TEMPLE AND KINGSHIP

Next to the land theme, both the sanctuary in which Yahweh was encountered in a special manner and the institution of the monarchy, had pivotal roles in the thought of the D historian. Each of these is a subject which can be examined in its own right, but they interplay at so many points that it is fruitful to discuss them together as well as to look at their individual features. The idea of the sanctuary puts us in touch with the historian's thinking about the worship of Yahweh and his particularized presence in Israel; the notion of the kingship opens up the broad political, social perspective in which the historian maintained a definite interest. Their interpenetration arises at the point where the king as political representative and the temple as religious center, meet both in reality and in the D historian's thinking.

THE TEMPLE

Scholars have long noted the preoccupation of the Book of Deuteronomy with the sanctuary of Yahweh. The key chapter is Deuteronomy 12, which speaks of "the place which the Lord your God will choose" (Deut. 12:5). The implication is understood readily, that this place is to be a single place out of all the places where Yahweh might be worshiped and where sacrifice might be offered to him. At this one place he will make his name dwell (Deut. 12:11), as if the D historian here were emphasizing that God is not confined to any circumscribed location on the earth (cf. 1 Kings 8:27) but approaches his people intimately through the disclosure of the holy name.

The special accent, however, is the centralization of the cult or worship at one sanctuary in Israel. What comes to mind immediately is the unusual role that Jerusalem played in the worship of Israel. From the time that David established this city as the center of his empire, only to have it consecrated through the construction of the temple by Solomon, down through the centuries until the Babylonian destruction, Jerusalem gained an increasingly important role. When the northern tribes seceded, they naturally firmed up their own cult centers, (1 Kings 12:26–30), all of which had older histories of usage. This multiplication of cult sites was a serious violation of the covenant in the eyes of the historian. Throughout his historical assessment, he looked back to see that it was this sin, committed by Jeroboam I in setting up the calves at Bethel and Dan, that finally initiated the internal disintegration of Israel.

There were further events which contributed to his solicitude. It is likely that we cannot understand his viewpoint on the centralization of the cult at Jerusalem without grasping the importance the collapse of the northern kingdom in 721 B.C. had for him and his program. In the wake of the disaster of the Assyrian invasion of the North, the fundamental religious and cultic traditions underwent a time of crisis. With no firmly operating centers any longer functioning in the North, with the various religious groups having experienced dispersion just as the common people, and with the general conditions of chaos in the North, a problem of some moment was how earlier traditions and institutions could be preserved for the future. We therefore see during the late eighth, and surely in the seventh century, a transposition of northern traditions into the framework of the still firmly grounded cult of Jerusalem in Judah. Many of the traditions, either by means of written form or oral transmission, were carried from North to South during this period, and in the process they were brought under the dominant viewpoint of the central sanctuary and its priesthood.

It has often been pointed out that the D history contains many traditions which at one time had their home in the North. There are those concerning Shechem, such as in Joshua 24, or the traditions about Shiloh and the ark which are at the heart of the Samuel story (1 Sam. 1—4). We have already noted numerous cases in which the historian used traditions with an older history. Not a small amount of this must have been channeled to the South from the northern kingdom following the latter's demise.

Precisely here emerges an important fact regarding the central role of Jerusalem in the historian's theology. The study of some of the traditional material employed by the historian shows that he did not initiate the idea of a single place at which Yahweh was to be met in worship, but rather incorporated into his work archaic material about old cult places. Shiloh and Shechem are examples of this. The study of these older traditions shows that these cult sites apparently also played a central role in ancient Israel, just as Jerusalem was to do in the thinking of the historian. In fact, there is a tendency in recent scholarship to see such central cult centers as Shechem or Shiloh as connected with the tribal unification (Josh. 18:1), so that a particular cult place would exemplify the bond shared by a group of tribes. The note in Judges 21:19, that an annual feast was made for Yahweh at Shiloh, is illustrative of the important role this site had in the premonarchic era.

The absence of a specific name of a site in the important chapter on centralization (Deut. 12) might suggest that the readers of the historian's work would know that he was referring to Jerusalem. However, it is also possible that the crux of the chapter is not so much fixing upon Jerusalem as the one place, but on the idea of a single place anywhere and in any period as being important for maintaining Israel's covenant bond. In other words, Deuteronomy 12 might be laying out the basic theology of the D historian regarding the dwelling place of Yahweh without confining its application to any one site. His intention here, then, might have been to set forth the fundamental principle by which Israel's fidelity could be measured at any period. In retrospect her tendency to veer away from the concept of unification and centralization by allowing localized Canaanite practices to persist in towns and villages, was clearly a factor in her eventual downfall. From the earliest times, Israel was seen to live under the obligation of a unity in her worship and concept of Yahweh, which openly would be symbolized by the one place at which she would assemble for her acts of sacrifice and devotion (Deut. 12:13).

In any case, what lay behind this concern of the historian was the widespread assimilation of cult practices from Canaanite centers which apparently were still being operated in a number of places during the eighth and seventh centuries B.C. In fact, it is this situation more than any other, that provides the social setting of the D historian's work as a whole and explains his dominant theological view.

The prevalence of extant Canaanite practices occurs in each of the books presently belonging to his overall work. The Book of Deuteronomy makes it evident from the beginning that the elimination of the cultic practices deriving from their Canaanite neighbors is the heaviest stricture put on Israel (Deut. 12:2–3). Joshua's speech incorporates an admonition along similar lines (Josh. 23:7–8). But no sooner have the people entered the land than the threatening symbiosis takes place. Israel is seen by the historian as having given in to the temptations of foreign worship (Judg. 2:11–13). The age of David seems to have been subjected less to such tendencies, although Solomon's age became more ambiguous (1 Kings 11:4). The entire period following the latter king was one in which rampant syncretism was carried on, according to the historian. His special interest in the account of Elijah's contest on Mount Carmel (1 Kings 18) is symptomatic in this regard.

It was all the more important for him, in view of all this, that the young reformer, King Josiah, rose upon the throne of Judah. The D historian's interest in Josiah and his reforming activity is present in numerous places, especially in the books of Kings, and it left its imprint upon his entire redactional labors. We have noted already the important section in 1 Kings 13:1–5, which in the form of a prediction mentions the rise of Josiah and his activity of tearing down the foreign altars. When Josiah does actually come to the throne, he enacts the very things which the D historian would most like to see him do. While holding the recently discovered Book of the Covenant (2 Kings 22:8–10), and standing beside a pillar in the house of the Lord at Jerusalem (2 Kings 23:1–3) he committed himself to keep all its statutes.

The activity of reform, which Josiah carried out, was that in which the D historian had his deepest concern. It was Josiah who deposed the non-Israelite priests, who destroyed the *asherim*, who eliminated the temple prostitution, and who carried out the widespread program of reform described in 2 Kings 23:4–20. Concomitantly it was this king who finally brought to realization the ideal of a unification of Israelite cultic practice, such as the Passover observance at the Jerusalem temple (2 Kings 23:21–23). Although even this reform would eventually fail in averting destruction, its impact upon the historian was considerable. Without a doubt he was a devoted supporter of the reform, and the tensions of this period left their impact upon his work as a whole.

The idea of a single place where Yahweh was to be approached in worship became a necessity in the thinking of the historian. For it was only in this way that unified belief and practice could be assured, that the integrity of the commitment itself could be guarded, and that finally the obligations of the covenant could be successfully carried out. The historian saw this ideal as one which ought indeed to have been fostered by those in charge of the cult—priests and other functionaries—but it was the king especially who was responsible for protecting the purity of the worship and obedience of Yahweh. Just at this point arises that steady stream of Deuteronomic condemnations which inevitably follow the narrative about the reigns of the kings of Israel and Judah in the books of Kings.

The historian argues that had Israel, and especially her kings, followed throughout a practice of consolidating her commitment at one place, had she rejected the centrifugal and disintegrative forces which an allowance of competing cult practices brought with them, her entire history would have gone differently. She might then have attained to that kind of ideal expressed in the prayer attributed to Solomon at the dedication of the temple (1 Kings 8:20–53). This prayer is in many ways a remarkable exhibit of the D historian's theology of the temple. It is unique in the first place because the historian was able to incorporate the reality of a temple structure into the commitment of Yahweh. In an environment in which temples and sanctuaries were an essential part of a society and commonly reflected the house or dwelling of a god, the historian was able to negotiate his way around dangers to the spirit of Yahwism. His "theology of the name," which he associated with the Jerusalem temple, was important here. The temple was not indispensable for Yahweh's dwelling with his people (2 Sam. 7:4–11); it was here that he made his name to dwell (1 Kings 8:29). In reality Yahweh's true home was in the heavens, and even these could not contain him (1 Kings 8:27).

On the matter of the temple conceived as a dwelling place, therefore, the historian could protect himself against unacceptable conceptions. More important for him was the temple in its ethical and relational aspects. Here is where Israel could turn to meet her God, both in the depth of obligation to the relationship and in his forgiving and restoring power when she would repent (1 Kings 8:46–53). It is apparent, then, that the historian connected the existence of the temple with the larger challenges of covenant loyalty. In bringing these together, the temple could no longer be simply a place where the mystery of God was to be encountered. It was the crucial focus for the special relation of Israel to Yahweh in every regard. Whether she experienced lack of rain, famine, or the risks of warfare (1 Kings 8:35–45), in all of these the prayer of Solomon petitions both for the upholding of her strength, and for deep instruction in the ways of her God (1 Kings 8:36, 39–40, 43).

Thus, as the Jerusalem sanctuary moved to the fore of the historian's thought, it was natural that it would influence his presentation in major ways. One example of this can be seen in his exposition concerning the two and one-half tribes east of the Jordan in Joshua 22. Having returned to the east after helping their fellow Israelites attain territories west of the river, the Transjordan tribes built an altar for themselves. It is described as a large altar, constructed near the Jordan River (Josh. 22:10). Upon hearing of this act, the tribes west of the Jordan become angered and threaten war against the eastern tribes. Finally, the matter is settled when the east Jordan tribes convince their western kinsmen that they have not acted out of malice, but in order that they and the generations after them might continue to revere Yahweh. This reverence would continue even though they might be separated in distance from Cisjordan and the central place of worship there (Josh. 22:21–34). The D historian's special interests appear in Joshua 22:16–20, where the act of building an altar in Transjordan is interpreted as a treacherous and rebellious deed. Ironically, as often happens in the way the historian uses his sources, he allows the statement to stand at the end, that the western tribes concurred in the altar which was now named "witness" (Josh. 22:34).

KINGSHIP

It is interesting now to turn to the subject of kingship in the historian's thought and to see how his concerns with this institution parallel those devoted to the temple. As the older sources which the historian employs make evident, the establishment of kingship in ancient Israel did not come about without considerable controversy. A source which the historian incorporated in Judges 9 attests to negative attitudes toward an early attempt at monarchy (Judg. 9:22–25). Alongside this account is one sometimes referred to as the Late Source, which takes overall a condemnatory position in relation to the establishment of a king over Israel (1 Sam. 8:10–22; 12:19).

Although these accounts do not derive from the D historian, they were not wholly foreign to his way of thinking. He, too, could see how the successive kings of Israel and Judah had failed to provide the kind of governance and motivation for the people to exemplify the ideals of the covenant. Nonetheless, this judgment appears in his work right alongside an opposite view, that the kingship was indeed a positive promise from Yahweh with far-reaching implications.

A difficult chapter to assess in respect to the historian's basic work, 2 Samuel 7 exhibits various features of his work. It is characterized by a similar flow and redundancy to sections confidently attributed to the historian. However, the chapter is not a clear replication of Deuteronomic style and thought, and it is probably safer to view it as stemming from sources very close to his own program rather than from his own hand. Nevertheless, this chapter reflects positively what the historian himself believed about the Davidic kingship.

The central motif in the oracle of Nathan to David in 2 Samuel 7 is the confirmation of the eternal promise to David and his house. This is achieved by a literary play on the idea of "building a house." First, it is David who approaches Nathan with the desire to build the house for Yahweh (vv. 2–3); Nathan's reply is that far from needing a house for himself, Yahweh will establish David's house into the future (v. 11). Without a doubt, this notion was a formative one for the D historian and served in no small way to provoke the anguish implied in his lengthy history. It is not too much to say that the idea of eternal promise to David's house was a fixed point for the historian —a cardinal, doctrinal focus by which much of Israel's history could be understood. This promise to David helped to unify other notions as well—notions such as Israel's being planted on her own land, disturbed no more, and free from the power of enemies who formerly afflicted her life (v. 10).

For the historian, then, the idea of kingship in Israel was insepa-
rable from the Davidic ideal. His work devoted an extraordinary
amount of space to the period of David, the basic theme of the two
books of Samuel which continued even into the early part of 1 Kings.
This period was one filled with special significance, especially for
understanding the vocation of Israel. Here are to be found some of
the reasons which help explain the historian's preoccupation with
kingship. We do not find him glorifying the institution in itself as
though it came down from heaven as a gift from the divine world.
The Davidic kingship is not ascribed cosmological or ontological
significance. Rather, its origin is in a voluntary act of election at a
moment in time. Not greatly different from other people such as
prophets (Amos 7:15), David was taken from tending the sheep
(1 Sam. 16:11), that is, under particular circumstances in history.
This selection of David to embody a new form of Yahweh's governance over his people is viewed as another gracious act in a series of
saving deeds for Israel which began in Egypt (2 Sam. 7:6).

One of the intriguing features of the historian's sources is the can-
dor of the description of David's reign. In the old stories involving
the conflict between Saul and David in 1 Samuel 18—31, David is
often described as cunning and even opportunistic (1 Sam. 27:1—
28:2). Even more realistic is the remarkable document included in
2 Samuel 9:1—20:26 and 1 Kings 1:1—2:46, the so-called Succession History of David. Here David is depicted not as the paragon of
perfection in respect to kingship, but with the weaknesses, defects,
and reprehensible actions which characterized some of his career.
This material is not from the hand of the D historian, but it is noteworthy how he could incorporate it alongside his theologized concept
of the Davidic ideal. At the same time, it should be noted that it is
presented under a scheme which either belongs to the historian or
was notably close to his own convictions: the notion of David under
the curse.[10] That David should have found himself under such a word
of chastisement following his relation to Bathsheba and complicity
in the death of Uriah (2 Sam. 12:11–12), was surely consonant with
the theological judgment of the historian.

Nevertheless, it is notable that explicit condemnation by the historian of David's reign is lacking. David sometimes is described as

having done things which, had they been done by one of the later kings, would surely have merited a negative evaluation from the historian. But there is a single, fundamental reason why this ideal king could not have fallen under such judgment. It was David who consolidated Israel's political strength against her neighbors in extraordinary ways. It was David who finally pressured the large, Canaanite cities such as Megiddo, Taanach, and others, into concurring with Israelite control of Cisjordan. Interestingly, this development receives some clarification through the archaeological finds of the tenth century B.C. It was also David who overcame the Jebusites and established Jerusalem as the new center (2 Sam. 5) and who brought the old cultic ark to its resting place in Jerusalem (2 Sam. 6).

Thus, rather than having given in to native religious elements in Cisjordan, David came—often inadvertently—to assume the role of the purger of features inimical to commitment to Yahweh. Through his broad, successful political activity he was able to establish a kingdom with the marks of internal unity (2 Sam. 5:1–4), of freedom from external threat (2 Sam. 5:6–25; 8:1–18; 10:1–19; 12:26–31), as well as prepare the way for an Israel united in her single devotion to Yahweh. Even though this achievement was marred by sporadic rebellions in his kingdom (2 Sam. 15—19), these did not offset the devotion of later memory concerning David's accomplishments. In that devotion the D historian was a singularly ardent participant.

For the historian, however, the Davidic ideal was not long to be carried on as a reality in Israel. Altogether it does not appear that he was as positively inclined toward David's successor, Solomon, although the latter lived in the afterglow of David's successes. The historian's treatment of Solomon is mixed. On the one hand, the hopes for Solomon's reign, attributed to David as his last words to Solomon (1 Kings 2:1–4), as well as the prayer for wisdom (1 Kings 3:6–9), reflect the historian's ideas. But the realities of Solomon's reign countered such expectations in uncomfortable ways. At the end of it all, the Deuteronomic disappointment is stated in the judgment that Solomon had not kept the covenant (1 Kings 11:11–14), and that the tragic division of the kingdom would come soon as a judgment in the face of his failure.

From the times of Solomon onward, the Davidic kingship is reckoned by the historian not so much according to its promise, but rather according to the repeated failures regarding its realization. Neither in the separated northern kingdom of Israel nor in Judah were there examples of successful realization of these expectations. In the historian's evaluation only two lights illuminate the largely dark picture of the period of the divided monarchy. The first to earn approval is Hezekiah of Jerusalem (715–687 B.C.) for his attention to the prophet Isaiah and for his reforming activity (2 Kings 18:1—20:21). The second was Josiah (640–609 B.C.) whose policies of reformation in regard to the historian's thought have been discussed previously. Apart from these two kings, the Davidic hope remained just that, an ideal awaiting embodiment. In contrast to the prophets who could envision a future fulfillment in which the ideal of the Davidic kingdom would be realized, the historian attempted to explain how one of the most cherished promises given to Israel had fallen short of realization.

Temple and kingship, then, are two intertwined components associated with Jerusalem. Through each of these institutions Yahweh offered his protective presence to Israel. Yet neither was a gift apart from the call to responsibility. Each could be seen in its depth only by means of its grounding in the covenant. The ideal would become reality when the king, giving himself in genuine fidelity to Yahweh's covenant, would bring all things into a unity at the one place where Yahweh would cause his name to dwell. This would happen when the threatening elements of Canaanite practice, still so prevalent in the land, would be rejected and eliminated. It would happen when the fragmentation of worship and commitment would be overcome by a joyful celebration of all of Israel's feasts at the one place now overriding all others (Deut. 16:1–17). It would happen when the king himself, as first among his people, would find his strength in "walking in his ways and keeping his statutes, his commandments, his ordinances, his testimonies, as written in the law of Moses" (1 Kings 2:3).

CHAPTER NINE

THE FUTURE

It was in the face of the devastating events of the late seventh and early sixth centuries B.C., that the D historian set about to compose his work. The times were bleaker than any experienced previously by the people of Judah. Even the conditions once faced by her ancestors in Egypt, now only a memory reaffirmed through regularized ceremonies, could scarcely be held up in comparison with the experience of collapse and abandonment which the invasion of a strong Babylonian army produced. The period was one of major crisis forever leaving its imprint on the consciousness of Judaism. Judah referred to it as the "exile" (*gālût*). For later generations which did not live through the events, the term could gloss over the anguished realities which accompanied the shaking, and even loss, of all foundations.

In that anguish the historian himself participated. But more than this, apparently behind his masterful work there lies an effort to explain historically and theologically the brute facts of disarray and confusion in his people's existence. Throughout the reading of his work a poignant question comes to mind again and again. Is it a sympathetic soul which shines through the elaborate program of organization, composition, and redaction in the historian's work? Since there are numerous tracings of foolish and stubborn decisions, which led ineluctably to disaster, are we to conclude that he saw events primarily in the form of doom and death? Or does there also lie behind the work the spirit of one who has not altogether abandoned hope? Is there within the historian's presentation evidence for what he thought and believed about this future?

In this chapter the contention is set forth that there is an aspect of hopefulness to be found in the historian. It is not to be located in explicit references in his work. Rather it is perceivable in the basic form of his presentation and in his work as such, which attempts to look backward, to trace through the threads of a complicated history.

The very fact of the historian's effort is itself an item worthy of inquiry. Although it is evident from his own occasional remarks that he derived his material from chronicles or archives, it is equally clear that his work was not intended as a mere deposit of facts about Israel's history. The historian undertook the task of composing his work with certain deeply-felt concerns in mind. As a broader kind of response to the problem, however, it would appear that the historian's fundamental interest was to search out and bring about a change in the conditions which led his people to where they were at the time of his writing.

The detailed, backward look characterizing the D history, is one projected from a particular moment in time, the crisis leading to the exile. Insofar as the exile was a crushing experience of abandonment and punishment, it was organically related to the past history of Israel's relationship with Yahweh. The disastrous events of the exilic age did not happen simply as a historical accident. They were the outcome of a cumulative condition of guilt in Israel. To trace the history of Israel's rejections leading to the disaster became the overarching plan of the historian. Apparently by carrying out such as task he could envision a breakthrough, both in Israel's understanding and accompanying willingness to change, as well as in the divine response to a disobedient people.

At least such an interpretation is worth testing. It is particularly worthwhile to try out its validity in respect to the way the historian ends his work in 2 Kings 25:27–30. We might assume that as he arrives at his final summary of Israel's history, following the long course he has traced, some indication of his final assessment might shine through. Such is not the case, at least not in an explicit manner. Nonetheless, the last two chapters of his history are instructive, and the idiosyncracies of the ending in 2 Kings 25 can be explained.

The final chapters of 2 Kings (24—25) are characterized by simplicity and directness. Evidently the D historian used the sources at his disposal, adding his own comments only in 2 Kings 24:3–4, 9, 19–20. For the rest the description is apparently a quite accurate reflection of the double siege of Jerusalem, first during the reign of

Jehoiachin, who was deported in 597 B.C., and in a second attack during the reign of Zedekiah ten years later. The narrative descriptions of this chapter can be set next to the diary of daily entries made by the recorders of Nebuchadnezzar's conquests in the so-called "Babylonian chronicle."[11] The overthrow of Jerusalem and the beginning of Judah's exile are two of the more successfully documented events of the Old Testament, having received this kind of supportive evidence from Babylonian texts.

These chapters stand out as unusual. The bare presentation of events without comment is unique in the historian's work. We might ask why, of all places, he refrained from making his own extensive evaluation of what had happened. Here at the end, with Judah now under serious chastisement, we might have expected a lengthy discourse composed once more by the historian for the purpose of setting into proper light the reason things had come to their present state. No such explanation is given. Even more remarkably, his great work draws to a close with only the briefest note in 2 Kings 25:27–30, that some years later Jehoiachin was released from his confinement and treated amicably by Evil-merodach, king of Babylon. The unclimactic ending is reminiscent of the ending of the narrative of the Book of Acts in the New Testament (Acts 28:30–31) which similarly closes with a direct statement, leaving unanswered many questions about the outcome of all that has preceded.

A number of explanations might be made for the curt ending of 2 Kings 25. One is that it is a characteristic of Hebrew narrative to stretch the components of a story across a horizontal span, allowing the simple narration itself to provide the tension and climax of what is described. In this case our difficulties with the short ending may reflect our modern paradigms of literary formation rather than point to anything out of order in the historian's sudden ending of his work. Looked at in this way it might not be unusual that a final Deuteronomic summary is lacking. Perhaps a reduction to the sparsest description reflected the best of Hebrew narrative, and in the final redaction of this work the description was left to stand with this lack of extended comment.

However, a literary explanation alone does not do ample justice to the interpretation of the final section of the historian's work. His candid use of bare details about the attack on Jerusalem in 2 Kings 25:8–17 suggests a theological explanation as well. The historian himself has made clear from the earliest part of his work that the word of challenge lies upon the house of Israel. We have seen this in the sense of obligation imposed by the covenant and by the reality of threats and curses which hover over Israel as a constant reminder and motivation. In recording the simple facts of the attack upon Jerusalem, the historian intimates that the curse has been thrown into effect. And yet this is done with no flare. The bare recording of the incidents of final catastrophe lets the message come across more effectively than any moralizing would have accomplished. Thus the whole of 2 Kings 25 might be said to have made use of this technique. If the final four verses of the work belong to the latest redaction, they follow the style of presentation that the historian himself has incorporated up to 2 Kings 25:26.

Are there possibilities that the historian could view these events as the basis for a new beginning, a regeneration through fire, turning Israel toward an unknown future? Surely that is what many of the tragic events of the past meant for him. We have noted the presence of such a scheme in the Book of Judges, in which Israel's apostasy is followed by chastisement, then by repentance, and finally by Yahweh's return to save his people from destruction. That cycle does not cease with the judges, for after Saul there arises David and a new era of deliverance. Even the dark days of the kings in both Israel and Judah are intersected by rays of hope—in the reforms of Hezekiah and Josiah. Yet it would have to be recalled that the historian knew of a northern kingdom wiped out for over a century by the time he began his work. Perhaps the same dark future as obtained in the North would also come about in the South. And perhaps the cumulative effect of Israel's disobedience and the heinous activities of Manasseh meant that the old pattern of disaster followed by relief could no longer be taken for granted. The possibility of an unrelieved punishment and rejection no doubt lay before him.

Judging from other works contemporary with that of the historian, the question of radical abandonment by Yahweh was evidently an urgent one for those experiencing the days leading to exile and beyond. There are indications in the Book of Jeremiah, for example, that confidence in Yahweh's power to deliver in the face of these events had waned in the hearts of some of this prophet's contemporaries, who began to look to other sources of help (Jer. 44:18). The destruction of the city was at the hands of a great outpouring of divine wrath (Lam. 2:2–3), and for some that thought led to despair. Even during the exile itself, the strong apologetic tone of a document like Second Isaiah betrays at many points the collapse of belief which must have been the experience of many of his hearers (Isa. 46:3–13).

The responses on the part of different groups to the extremities of this period were varied. The options open to people of this time included a number of possible reactions. Some might interpret the events of the calamity as a total forsaking by Yahweh of his people, an end to the covenant bond that had bound them in the past. Others might have found the pressure of events an excuse for seeking more effective gods, as we have noted in some of the contemporaries of Jeremiah. Still others might have clung to the message that Yahweh had not forsaken his people with finality, but that there was room for salvation oracles such as those delivered by Second Isaiah or Ezekiel.

Within such a framework the D historian is distinctive in his viewpoint. His work ends neither with a clear-cut basis for any kind of continuing hope for Judah nor with an embittered finale of doom. His last words of Israel's history are a simple presentation of the facts of Jerusalem's destruction and of Jehoiachin's later release. Could it be that for the historian those details contained dim forewarnings of a new era in which Yahweh would act for his people? The D historian leaves that possibility open, but in suspense.

In any case, when this work is considered as a whole, there emerges one fact which has been alluded to several times. The historian undertook his work to trace out the course of decisions and events which involved Israel in her tragic disobedience. His intent was not to present a glorified version of Israel's history, recounting it so that Israel could come out looking unblemished. Rather he told it as straightforward as possible, presenting his own judgments at many places. Yet more than this, he seems to have undertaken his work for a purpose, affecting finally the question whether he could still entertain a hope for Israel in the bleak days of disaster and exile.

That purpose has been described by one Old Testament scholar as an effort to compose a historical work in the form of a comprehensive public confession of sins.[12] That interpretation is a plausible one. It means that by laying out the details of Israel's history of disobedience the historian could conceive of his work as an effective act of corporate penitence in the eyes of Yahweh, the God of Israel. Its effect might be that associated with various postexilic prayers, the intent of which was to initiate a renewed relationship between God and his people. Usually these prayers concentrate on the justice of God in punishing his people, thereby implying that Yahweh's glory is upheld even in the face of the rebellions of his people. If the D history reflects such an intention, then the facts of Israel's sinfulness are laid out as a way of confessing the justice of God, even in the night of her present punishment. Having recognized that, however, the historian could also assume that what remains of Israel in the aftermath of the disaster could become the grounds for a new beginning, and that Yahweh himself would be moved through such public confession to remember his covenant and to intervene on behalf of his people.

Although it might be tempting to interpret the sudden termination of the D historian's work as an expression of despair, it is probably more correct to assume that he could not have set aside lightly the expectation of a continued care for Israel by the God of her ancient covenant. How that God would be able to begin anew with the reality of so much disarray, the historian could scarcely see. But that he would do so is implied not so much by the terse ending of his work, as by the structure and intent of the work as a whole. As a result of an often evil past, the future was shrouded in bewildering uncertainty. Yet other experiences in that past could lead the historian to conclude that for Israel there would be a future.

CHAPTER TEN

THE IMPACT OF THE D HISTORY

In summing up the D history, it remains for us to inquire regarding its influence on other periods and to make some suggestions concerning its significance for our own time. In some important ways all parts of scripture cast their rays out over later periods, influencing people in the ways they approach problems. The D history seems to have been unusual in this regard, for the books that comprise it are some of the most quoted texts used in later circles of both Judaism and Christianity.

It seems as though the impact of the D history extended in two significant directions during later periods. The first was in the way later circles carried out their exegesis of earlier texts, akin to the manner in which the historian had begun to handle older sources. The second was through a more comprehensive influence from the D history on the theological understandings of the ensuing periods.

There can be little question but that the formulations of the D history were greatly emulated during the period following the exile. Beginning in the sixth century B.C. and following into the succeeding two centuries, there is discernible a tradition of public recital of sins which clearly reflects Deuteronomic forms. One such recital attributed to Ezra is found in Nehemiah 9:6–37. Following the historian's distinctive form, the prayer of Ezra abounds with references to earlier events of Israel's history. Its earnest confession is done with the specific intention of turning away the divine wrath by an acknowledgment of his justice in the face of Israel's iniquities and her punishment.

The model prayer attributed to Daniel in Daniel 9:4–19 abounds similarly in expressions which are Deuteronomic. Due to the fact that much of Daniel 7—12 hardly can be dated earlier than the times of

Antiochus IV Epiphanes (175–163 B.C.), we can conclude that this prayer reflects a persistence of Deuteronomic motifs right through to the second century B.C. Again we find in this prayer the same emphasis on the sins of Israel, the recognition of God's justice in bringing punishment, and the petitioning for the turning of his wrath from the city of Jerusalem. The fact that Jerusalem is so central and that its debasement is lamented in a special way, points again to Deuteronomic features. Since what comes as a response to this prayer is the astonishing revelation of the seventy weeks of years (Dan. 9:20–27), we can assume that just this kind of prayer, representing the normative, correct form, could elicit the appropriate answer from the divine world. That answer is given to Daniel through the medium of Gabriel.

These prayers, as well as others in the aprocryphal writings such as 2 Esdras 3:4–36 and 8:20–36, or Baruch 1:15—3:8, attest how widespread was the impact of the Deuteronomic way of formulating public confession of sin. Important always was the recital of the past, for it was in the voicing of the negative past that the possibilities for a new situation could arise in the present. What the D historian presented in his impressive work became the appropriate and common form through which penitence and the petitions for deliverance could be expressed.

Among the later community at Qumran, which produced the documents known as the Dead Sea scrolls, there existed a strong inspiration derived from the study of the Book of Deuteronomy and the D history as a whole. This is seen not only in the individual references taken from some part of the D history, but it is evident even more in the freely dispersed Deuteronomic ideas which have been incorporated at many points into the community's self-understanding.[13] Understandably they have merged with other basic notions of the community's ideology, but in the process originally Deuteronomic ideas have been elevated to a new level. Thus, for example, the fundamental eschatological beliefs of the community provide a new dimension to older Deuteronomic ideas, even while the latter supply much of the framework for Qumran eschatology.

It is possible to go so far as to say that the community at Qumran conceived of itself as a society which was attempting to realize the sort of purity and commitment so integral to the D historian's picture of an ideal Israel. Thus the Manual of Discipline, which defines the identity of the community and its special life style, is heavily saturated with Deuteronomic ideas about the devotion of members to the commandments and ordinances of Yahweh. At the same time it focuses sharply on an intentional separation from the works of the sons of evil, who may be taken as an eschatologized version of the "foreign peoples" in the D historian's work. It is noteworthy that the Manual of Discipline also carries in its rubrics a form of typical Deuteronomic confession: the Levites who lead the community in its liturgies are "to rehearse the iniquities of the children of Israel." Other documents of the sect, such as the one recounting the war between the sons of light and the sons of darkness, express Deuteronomic motifs, again within the framework of a deep, eschatological consciousness.

The New Testament writers use the Book of Deuteronomy and other parts of the D history as favorite sources for direct quotation. It has been noted frequently that the three words which Jesus quotes to the tempter, according to the version in Matthew, are from the Book of Deuteronomy (Matt. 4:4, 7, 10; see Luke 4:4, 8, 12). Even more telling for an influence on the New Testament is the scheme of prophecy and fulfillment used in the gospels. This scheme is especially important in the Gospel of Matthew where we find often an introductory formula such as "This took place to fulfill what was written in X," followed by a direct quotation. It is at least evident that the basic scaffolding in this notion of prophecy and fulfillment has been influenced by the D historian's work.

In a previous chapter we have examined the relation between prophecy and fulfillment in the D history, noting how this scheme is employed throughout his work. There the word "fulfill" was seen to suggest a connection between an announcement in the face of earlier events which would find a fuller outcome at a later time. The prominence of the word "fulfill" in such books as Matthew suggests that the New Testament documents have taken over and transformed an old Deuteronomic formula into a basic Christological one. Now it is employed to show how earlier prophecies from the Old Testament can be applied to events in the life of Jesus. It is not in place for us to deal with the specifics of how this is done in the gospels. But the notion of prophecy and fulfillment, so important as an apologetic and proclamatory tool in the New Testament, owes in no small way its development to the D historian and his presentation of ancient Israelite history.

There was another sense in which the Deuteronomic thinking left its impact upon the later communities and their reflection. This was in its strong emphasis on challenge and commitment, particularly in respect to the covenant obligations. Although the D historian viewed the relation between Yahweh and Israel as a dynamic one, the obedience-obligation emphasis in the D historical work could come to play a role out of proportion to its intended place. When this happened, the theme of Yahweh's delivering power in the events happening to Israel would tend to take a less important place than previously. Now the communities would define their life and realize the divine will in their midst by means of a more legalized understanding of the relationship between God and his people. We can see this happening in the community at Qumran, as in later nomistic tendencies within Christianity, even to our own time. The Deuteronomic view was expressed so forcibly and stated so comprehensively and clearly, that it could not but catalyze a certain type of thinking in the later communities. The later appropriation of it did not degenerate into such nomistic interpretations, but kept itself open to the wider, historical framework of the work and to the correction and deepening that could come from other contributions, such as those of the prophets, wisdom, or the psalms. Thus, when the opposite occurred, the communities were forced into narrower positions which lessened their effectiveness and deprived them of their vitality.

As we draw this study to a close, a word should be said again about the D history as a source for present-day proclamation. There are rich resources in the historian's work, both among the older traditions which he incorporated and which he often left untouched, as well as in his own evaluations and interpretations which appear at so many points in his work. Present-day communities, to which sermons based on sections of this work might be addressed, will find the variety of historical, social, and political situations illuminating. The varied settings of the texts will often suggest similarities to issues confronted in our own times, thus increasing their applicability. An imaginative handling of the texts which combines historical work with contemporary awareness, will enliven the process of interpretation.

It is important, however, to recall a basic point made several times in this study. The D history must be interpreted as a wholistic work. As we have seen, this history pretends to be no less than a comprehensive evaluation of Israel from the past to the present. That overview was grounded in a conviction of Israel's special election by a gracious God. It recognized her peculiar summons to accountability, not shying away from the reality of divine wrath in the face of failure and apostasy. It is in this larger framework that the emphasis on laws and ordinances, and the tendency to exclusiveness occur. If that larger framework is left out of the picture, present-day communities will incline toward understanding the D history as a tract promoting legalistic and separatistic features which are foreign to the intention of the work and inimical to a fuller biblical perspective. If such fragmentation is avoided and the whole view of this history is preserved, the D history will yield abundant rewards to those courageous enough to speak from it, to those responsive to what it is able to address to us, and to any who may seek to understand how this impressively executed work of ancient Israel continues to challenge us today.

NOTES

1. The terms derive from Martin Noth and Ivan Engnell. For a discussion of their work see Norman H. Snaith, "The Historical Books," in H. H. Rowley, *The Old Testament and Modern Study* (Oxford: Clarendon, 1951), pp. 84–114.
2. Yigael Yadin, "Hazor," *Encyclopedia of Archeological Excavations in the Holy Land, Volume 2* (London: Oxford University, 1976), pp. 474–495.
3. Moshe Weinfeld, "The Period of the Conquest and of the Judges as seen by the Earlier and the Later Sources," *Vetus Testamentum* 17 (1967): 93–113.
4. Gerhard von Rad, *Studies in Deuteronomy*, Studies in Biblical Theology, No. 9 (London: SCM, 1953), pp. 74–91.
5. William L. Moran, "The Ancient Near East Background of the Love of God in Deuteronomy," *Catholic Biblical Quarterly* 25 (1963): 77–87.
6. Martin Noth, "For all who rely on works of the law are under a curse," *The Laws in the Pentateuch and other Studies*, trans. D. R. Ap-Thomas (Philadelphia: Fortress, 1967), pp. 118–131.
7. Walther Zimmerli, *The Law and the Prophets: A Study of the Meaning of the Old Testament*, trans. R. E. Clements (New York: Harper & Row, Torchbooks, 1965), pp. 46–60.
8. Delbert R. Hillers, *Treaty-Curses and the Old Testament Prophets*, Biblica et Orientalia, No. 16 (Rome: Pontifical Biblical Institute, 1964), p. 6.
9. Gerhard von Rad, "The Promised Land and Yahweh's Land in the Hexateuch," *The Problem of the Hexateuch, and Other Essays*, trans. E. W. Trueman Dicken (New York: McGraw-Hill, 1966), pp. 79–93.

10. R. A. Carlson, *David, the Chosen King* (Stockholm: Almqvist & Wiksell, 1964), pp. 131–246.

11. David Noel Freedman, "The Babylonian Chronicle," *Biblical Archaeologist* 19 (1956): 50–60.

12. Gerhard von Rad, *Old Testament Theology*, Vol. 1, trans. D. M. G. Stalker (New York: Harper & Row, 1962), pp. 342–343.

13. For examples see the translation of the Manual of Discipline in Theodore H. Gaster, trans., *The Dead Sea Scriptures*, rev. ed. (New York: Doubleday, Anchor Books, 1964), pp. 46–69.

SELECTED BIBLIOGRAPHY

ACKROYD, PETER R. *Exile and Restoration: A Study of Hebrew Thought of the Sixth Century B.C.* Philadelphia: Westminster, 1968.

————. *The First Book of Samuel.* Cambridge Bible Commentary. Cambridge: University, 1971.

BOLING, ROBERT G. *Judges.* The Anchor Bible, Vol. 6A. New York: Doubleday, 1975.

ELLUL, JACQUES. *The Politics of God and the Politics of Man.* Translated by Geoffrey M. Bromiley. Grand Rapids: Eerdmans, 1972.

GRAY, JOHN. *I & II Kings.* 2nd rev. ed. Philadelphia: Westminster, 1970.

HERTZBERG, HANS WILHELM. *I & II Samuel.* Translated by J. S. Bowden. Old Testament Library. Philadelphia: Westminster, 1964.

HILLERS, DELBERT R. *Covenant: The History of a Biblical Idea.* Baltimore: Johns Hopkins, 1969.

KENYON, KATHLEEN. *Royal Cities of the Old Testament.* New York: Schocken, 1971.

MCKENZIE, JOHN L. *The World of the Judges.* Englewood Cliffs: Prentice-Hall, 1966.

MALY, EUGENE H. *The World of David and Solomon.* Englewood Cliffs: Prentice-Hall, 1966.

MARTIN, JAMES D. *The Book of Judges.* Cambridge Bible Commentary. Cambridge: University, 1975.

MAYES, A. D. H. *Israel in the Period of the Judges.* Studies in Biblical Theology. Second Series, 29. London: SCM, 1974.

MILLER, J. MAXWELL and TUCKER, GENE M. *The Book of Joshua.* Cambridge Bible Commentary. London, New York: Cambridge University, 1974.

NOTH, MARTIN, "The Jerusalem Catastrophe of 587 B.C., and its significance for Israel," *The Laws in the Pentateuch and other Studies*. Translated by D. R. Ap-Thomas. Philadelphia: Fortress, 1967.

VON RAD, GERHARD. *Old Testament Theology*, Vol. 1. Translated by D. M. G. Stalker. New York: Harper & Row, 1962.

ROBINSON, J. *The First Book of Kings*. Cambridge Bible Commentary. Cambridge: University, 1972.

————. *The Second Book of Kings*. Cambridge Bible Commentary. London, New York, Cambridge: University, 1976.

SOGGIN, J. ALBERTO. *Joshua*. Old Testament Library. Philadelphia: Westminster, 1972.

WIFALL, WALTER. *The Court History of Israel: A Commentary on First and Second Kings*. St. Louis: Clayton, 1975.